ILENE COOPER

ELEANOR ROOSEVELT

FIGHTER FOR JUSTICE

HER IMPACT ON THE CIVIL RIGHTS MOVEMENT, THE WHITE HOUSE, AND THE WORLD

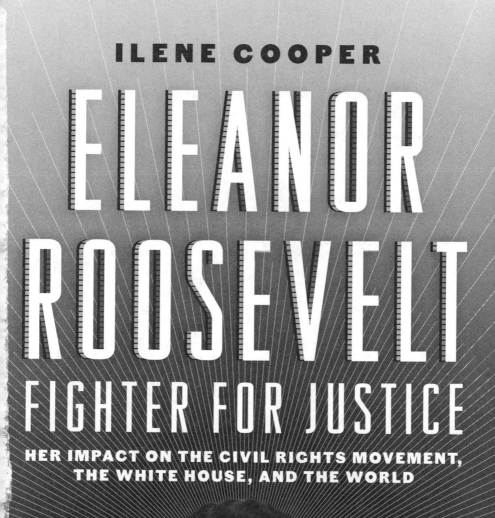

ABRAMS BOOKS FOR YOUNG READERS ★ NEW YORK

For Isabel Baker, Laura Bernstein, Jerry Eichengreen, Beth Elkayam, Susie Greenwald, and Phyllis Victorson, dear friends and strong women, each of whom works hard to make the world a better place

All photographs are courtesy of the Franklin D. Roosevelt Library and Museum, Hyde Park, New York, with the following exceptions:. pages 21, 91, 120, courtesy of the Library of Congress; page 112, courtesy of the National Archives.

Excerpts from "Address by Mrs. Franklin D. Roosevelt—the Chicago Civil Liberties Committee," page 158, courtesy of the Estate of Eleanor Roosevelt.

Library of Congress Cataloging-in-Publication Data
Names: Cooper, Ilene, author.
Title: Eleanor Roosevelt, fighter for justice / by Ilene Cooper.
Description: New York: Abrams Books for Young Readers, 2018. |
Includes bibliographical references and index.
Identifiers: LCCN 2017058795 | ISBN 9781419722950 (hardcover with jacket)Subjects:
LCSH: Roosevelt, Eleanor, 1884-1962—Juvenile literature. |
Presidents' spouses—United States—Biography—Juvenile literature. |
Civil rights movements—United States—History—20th century—Juvenile literature.
Civil rights workers—United States—Biography—Juvenile literature. | Women civil rights
workers—United States—Biography—Juvenile literature.
Classification: LCC E807.1.R48 C68 2018 | DDC 973.917092 [B]—dc23

Text copyright © 2018 Ilene Cooper
Book design by Sara Corbett

Printed and bound in USA
10 9 8 7 6 5 4 3 2 1

Abrams Books for Young Readers are available at special discounts when purchased in quantity for premiums and promotions as well as fundraising or educational use. Special editions can also be created to specification. For details, contact specialsales@abramsbooks.com or the address below.

ABRAMS The Art of Books
195 Broadway, New York, NY 10007
abramsbooks.com

CONTENTS

In June 1958, seventy-three-year-old Eleanor Roosevelt, a former First Lady of the United States, was driving through the hills of Tennessee. She was on her way to speak at the Highlander Folk School, an acquaintance at her side, a pistol near her hand. The gun was for protection. The Ku Klux Klan, one of the most dangerous hate groups in the United States, had placed a bounty on her head: $25,000 to kill Eleanor Roosevelt.

Eleanor, the widow of President Franklin Delano Roosevelt, was one of the most admired women in the world. She had earned that popularity by championing the causes of those who needed help getting the rights they deserved: the poor, women, immigrants, refugees. Eleanor's background was one of wealth and entitlement, yet emotionally, she knew what it was like to struggle. Her own insecurities translated into a desire to help others, but to turn her good intentions into action, she had to dig deep inside herself.

Perhaps her most controversial stand was her strong support of African Americans and their fight for civil rights. Many people in the United States turned their heads from the injustices—and the dangers—black people faced. Once she committed herself to the cause, Eleanor Roosevelt did not turn away. Turning away was not her style.

But as much as Eleanor was admired in some quarters, in others she was despised. From 1933 to 1945, when President Roosevelt died in office, Eleanor was a First Lady like no other. She didn't like staying at the White House presiding over luncheons and teas—although she did plenty of that, too—she had things to see, do, and fix. Those who disliked the president and his programs were also appalled that Eleanor had a life of her own—and one that involved being an outspoken advocate for the underdog at a time when prejudices were everywhere. After President Roosevelt died, during an unprecedented fourth term of the presidency, Mrs. Roosevelt kept on fighting injustice.

The Highlander Folk School in Monteagle, Tennessee, where Mrs. Roosevelt was headed that June day, had a decades-long history of working for social change in the country. During the 1950s, activists like Rosa Parks and Martin Luther King Jr. attended sessions on nonviolent protest there. The school had invited Mrs. Roosevelt to speak as part of a civil rights program about ways to protest unfair and immoral social conditions. She probably thought her visit to the Highlander School would just be another of the dozens of speaking engagements she made every year. But then the FBI advised her that a secret informant had told the agency that the Klan intended to stop the speech "even if they had to blow the place up."

The longtime head of the Federal Bureau of Investigation, J. Edgar Hoover, was no friend of Mrs. Roosevelt. He thought she was a dangerous liberal, and he ordered the FBI to follow her activities, bug her phone conversations, and keep a file on what she said and what was written about her. This dossier was begun in 1940, and by the time of her death in 1962, it was more than three thousand pages long!

When the FBI gave Mrs. Roosevelt the news of the threat against her life, they also informed her that if she decided to speak at the Highlander Folk School they could not protect her. Whether they couldn't—or wouldn't—Eleanor Roosevelt understood that if she made the trip to rural Tennessee, she would be on her own. The situation was dangerous, but she believed in the Highlander Folk School's mission and the cause of the civil rights movement.

So to Tennessee she went, determined as usual, but this time with a gun at her side.

ANNA HALL WAS THE BELLE OF HER DEBUTANTE SEASON.

GRANNY

Poor little rich girl. If ever a child fit that description, it was young Eleanor Roosevelt.

She was born on October 11, 1884 into a very privileged world. Her mother, Anna Hall, and her father, Elliott Roosevelt, came from wealthy families that were pillars of New York society. Eleanor's early years were lived in city town houses with fashionable addresses and country homes on expansive grounds. She was surrounded by servants and wore dresses made of velvet and lace. There were sea voyages, pony cart rides, plenty of dolls and toys. But one thing Eleanor didn't have: her mother's affection.

"My mother was one of the most beautiful women I have

ever seen," wrote Eleanor as the opening sentence of her autobiography. This was not just the opinion of an impressionable little girl. Anna Hall Roosevelt, graceful and with striking patrician features, was considered to be one of the great beauties of her day.

Anna's family was among the early arrivals in the country that would eventually become the United States of America. One relative helped draft the Declaration of Independence. Another, in 1787, signed the United States Constitution.

The family of Elliott Roosevelt also had roots in America that were deep and wealthy. Elliott was handsome and personable, and as a boy, it seemed as if he would go far. His older brother, Theodore, was a sickly child who suffered with asthma, so it was Elliott who came first in sports and games.

But then something changed. Theodore decided to exercise and strengthen his body. As he grew stronger, Elliott seemed to become weaker, and he began suffering from all sorts of nervous ailments. By the time they were young men, Theodore took his place as the leader of his family—and eventually of the country. Theodore Roosevelt went on to become the twenty-sixth president of the United States. Elliott devoted his life to good times, travel, dances, and drinking. Lots of drinking.

Still, when Anna Hall and Elliott Roosevelt decided to marry—Anna, only nineteen, Elliott, twenty-three—it seemed like an excellent match: shimmering stars from the same cloistered social circle, a joining of two distinguished families, both partners with enough resources to have a life of style and ease.

Ten months after their 1883 wedding, Eleanor was born. For Elliott, she was "a miracle from heaven." Perhaps Anna had thought that at first, but by the time Eleanor was two, she had given her little daughter a less-than-flattering nickname: Granny. It was a name, Eleanor would say, that made her want to "sink through the floor in shame."

Eleanor describes herself in her autobiography as a shy, solemn child who rarely smiled. This was not the sort of behavior that would have endeared her to Anna, who preferred charm and gaiety. She didn't understand her dour little daughter, and she was disappointed that Eleanor hadn't inherited her good looks. As an adult, Eleanor said that she knew she was "ugly," though photographs show a pleasant-looking, if plain, child. Nevertheless, her sense that her mother disapproved of her was a burden she carried throughout her life.

FIVE-YEAR-OLD ELEANOR AND
HER ADORING FATHER, ELLIOTT

Elliott, though, remained enchanted with his little daughter. Even after the birth of his sons, Elliott Jr. in 1889 and Hall in 1891, his daughter, whom he nicknamed Little Nell, remained his favorite. He loved spending time with her, and when he was away, he wrote her long letters about all the wonderful things they would do when they were together. It comforted and delighted her to receive notes from Elliott in which he remembered the trips they had already taken and offered promises of more: "through the Grand snow clad forests over the white hills, under the blue skies, as blue as those in Italy."

Her father became the center of Eleanor's world. "With my father," she remembered years later, "I was perfectly happy."

Anna, however, was not happy. The fairy-tale version of married life that had been predicted for her and Elliott turned out to be an illusion. It was not long into the marriage that Anna began to suspect that Elliott's drinking was a bigger problem than she could handle. His behavior was erratic, and his trips away, sometimes for pleasure, sometimes to attempt to break his addiction, bore holes into their family.

ELEANOR HAD A LIFELONG LOVE OF HORSES. HERE SHE'S AT GRANDMOTHER HALL'S SUMMER HOME IN TIVOLI, NEW YORK, IN 1894.

Eleanor didn't understand why her father was gone so often, but cherished the time they had together, much of it centered on their mutual love of horses and dogs. But on at least one occasion, Elliott took the opportunity to show Eleanor a very different side of life. Members of the upper classes were expected to be charitable to those less fortunate than themselves, and the Roosevelt family took their responsibility seriously. Both Elliott and his father, Theodore Sr., were supporters of a charity called the Children's Aid Society. One of the society's projects was providing places where the many young boys hawking newspapers on the streets of New York could sleep or get a hot meal for a small fee.

On Thanksgiving and Christmas, the boys enjoyed a free holiday dinner—turkey, ham, potatoes, and pie, the kind of food they rarely saw. One year, when Eleanor was about six, her father brought her to help serve a Thanksgiving dinner to scruffy boys with nicknames like Crutcher and Jake the Oyster at the Newsboys' Lodge. This was an eye-opening event for a little girl who lived in luxury.

Eleanor was also struck by her father's personal generosity. One night he left their house wearing his finest coat. He returned, shivering, his coat gone. Eleanor asked what had happened to it, and he told her he had given it to a "a small and ragged urchin" who needed the coat more than he did.

Through these experiences, and after attending other charitable functions with her family, Eleanor became aware that while her life was blessed with plenty, there were plenty of others who lived in poverty. These lessons, and the importance Elliott put on helping those less fortunate, were planted early and deep.

Wealth was not very helpful to Elliott Roosevelt, however. Each year his drinking became worse and his actions more outrageous. Anna tried to hold her household together while struggling with her own health issues. Then in 1892, while Elliott was away, she came down with a case of diphtheria, an infection that begins with a sore throat and headache. In Anna's case, it ended with death. She was twenty-nine years old.

AFTER ANNA'S DEATH IN 1892, THE CHILDREN'S ONLY PARENT WAS THE TROUBLED ELLIOTT.

It is telling that on hearing the news of her mother's death, Eleanor's first thought was that now her father would be coming home. And though he did return for the funeral, it had already been decided that his children would be best off living with Anna's mother, Eleanor's grandmother, Mary Hall. Eleanor later realized what a defeat this must have been for her father to be separated from her and the boys, to be seen as unable to care for his own children. But at the time, his eight-year-old daughter listened closely as he told her that someday she would make a home for him and they would travel the world together—"somehow it was always he and I."

This vision of life with her father (she wasn't quite sure where her brothers fit into the picture) helped sustain her when she moved into Grandmother Hall's large New York City brownstone home (in the summer, the family spent time at the Halls' country home in upstate New York, Tivoli). The household was dominated by Eleanor's young aunts and uncles, a rowdy crew in their late teens and twenties who always had drama happening in their lives. Grandmother Hall dealt with the chaos by going inside her bedroom and firmly closing the door.

Eleanor's brothers, five and seven years younger than she, didn't provide much company, and though her aunts and uncles were kind, they were focused on themselves. Eleanor spent a good deal of her free time living inside her head, spinning daydreams in which she was the heroine and her father was the hero.

In May of 1893, only six months after her mother died, there was another loss. Her brothers both came down with scarlet fever. She was sent to Tivoli so she wouldn't catch the illness, too. There, Eleanor received a telegram from her father telling her that though Hall was getting better, Elliott Jr. was gravely ill and would likely be joining Anna in heaven. The four-year-old died a few hours later.

A little more than a year later, the news was even worse. Nine-year-old Eleanor received the shocking announcement from her aunts that her father was dead. They did not tell her that he had died from complications after attempting suicide.

Eleanor remembered later that she wept and wept, but the following morning she returned to her dreamworld, where her father still lived. She was content to spend much of her time there. "I knew in my mind that my father was dead, and yet I lived with him more closely, probably than I had when he was alive."

The next five years were a difficult and lonely time for Eleanor. Already shy, now she became fearful—of the dark, of displeasing people, of failure. Her life revolved around school and the occasional outing. She also liked to read, and as she grew older, she was left alone to choose what she wanted from the extensive Hall library. That is, until her grandmother started asking questions about books she thought might be unsuitable for a girl of Eleanor's age—then they would disappear. That's what happened to Charles Dickens's *Bleak House*. Eleanor tried to find the novel for days.

A huge disappointment for Eleanor was her grandmother's decision to allow only occasional visits with her father's family, the Roosevelts. Being with her exuberant Uncle Teddy and his family was exhilarating and very outdoorsy—far different from what she was used to at her grandmother's house. But Grandmother Hall, having lost control of her own children, decided to be a stern disciplinarian with Eleanor and Hall. Eleanor described her grandmother's child-rearing theory this way: "We were brought up on the principle it was easier to say no than yes."

So it came as a surprise to Eleanor when she was fifteen that Grandmother Hall told her, "Your mother wanted you to go to boarding school in Europe, and I have decided to send you." It is more likely that Grandmother Hall felt that her children, often wild in their ways, could become a bad influence on Eleanor now that she was a teenager, and so she wanted Eleanor out of the house. "Suddenly life was going to change for me," Eleanor remembered.

She was to attend a school outside London, England, called Allenswood Academy. To leave behind the pain and sorrow of her early life was liberating for Eleanor, but she was also leaving every person and place she had ever known. She would be alone in a school across an ocean, and making new friends was something she did neither easily nor well. It must have taken every bit of strength she had to muster the courage to go. But by now Eleanor knew one thing about herself: "Anything I had accomplished had to be done across a barrier of fear."

2

FINDING HERSELF

After a long ocean voyage, "lost and lonely" fifteen-year-old Eleanor was dropped off at Allenswood Academy by an aunt. In her suitcase was a packet of her father's letters tied with ribbon. But Eleanor didn't have much time to feel sorry for herself. She had entered a dizzying new environment, and she quickly realized she needed to step up.

The headmistress at the girls' school was handsome, silver-haired Mademoiselle Marie Souvestre. She was the kind of woman whose "eyes looked through you," Eleanor later reflected, "and she always knew more than she was told." An avant-garde educator who taught her lessons with intensity

A FIFTEEN-YEAR-OLD ELEANOR AT THE TIME SHE WAS SENT TO ALLENSWOOD and enthusiasm and prized curiosity in her students, she was also a feminist who wanted her students to know that they could have happy, fulfilling lives, with or without marriage.

The women's movement—the push for women to have equal rights to men, including the right to vote—had been around for more than fifty years by the time Eleanor arrived at Allenswood in 1899. Most people in Eleanor's world were more comfortable with the status quo. Women, at least upper-class women, were raised to be helpmates to their husbands and mothers to their children. Even among the well-educated, few had careers.

Mlle. Souvestre had a different idea. She thought women and girls should be able to think for themselves, find ways to make a difference in the world, and she wanted to instill in them "courageous judgment, and . . . a deep sense of public duty." It was from Mlle. Souvestre, Eleanor later noted, that she learned one of her life's guiding principles: that the "underdog should always be championed."

Almost immediately upon her arrival at Allenswood, Eleanor became Mlle. Souvestre's favorite. One of the rules of the school was that French was the primary language to be spoken.

Eleanor's first nanny had been French, and so as a toddler she'd learned the language before learning English. This fluency gained Eleanor a coveted spot at Mlle. Souvestre's dinner table, where she spoke with her teacher in the woman's native tongue. She was also invited to her teacher's study with other select students to discuss—also in French—literature and poetry.

MADEMOISELLE MARIE SOUVESTRE
WAS ONE OF THE GREATEST INFLUENCES
ON THE LIFE OF ELEANOR.

Teacher and student, over the next three years, became exceptionally close. They traveled across Europe together, and Mlle. Souvestre, who was in her early seventies, left it to Eleanor to handle all the arrangements. Those responsibilities gave her a new sense of confidence. Eleanor was also thrilled by her teacher's spontaneity; Mlle. Souvestre readily threw away plans if something more interesting presented itself. After years of doing what she was told, the idea that decisions could be made according to what one found appealing was wonderfully liberating. "Never

again," she later wrote, "would I be the rigid little person I had
been theretofore."

There was one more thing that Eleanor learned from
Mlle. Souvestre. It might seem minor, but it went a long way
to boost the girl's confidence: She taught Eleanor how to
dress fashionably. For years Eleanor had been embarrassed
about her clothes. She had grown very tall very early, yet her
grandmother insisted that her skirts remain short, like
a child's, although the dresses of other girls swept the
floor. When she was finally allowed to dress more age appro-
priately, her clothes were usually made over from her aunts'
hand-me-downs.

Mlle. Souvestere frankly told Eleanor she didn't think
much of her clothes. While they were in Paris, she insisted
that her student have a dress made just for her. At first, Eleanor was doubtful. She had been taught to be frugal, but Mlle.
Souvestre wanted her to have a dress she'd be proud to wear.
A flattering, dark-red evening gown was made. Decades later,
Eleanor still remembered the joy she felt wearing that dress,
and thought fondly of it as the article of clothing that had
given her "more satisfaction than . . . any dress I have ever
had since."

ALLENSWOOD ACADEMY WAS A SCHOOL WITH THIRTY-FIVE STUDENTS, GIRLS BETWEEN THE AGES OF THIRTEEN AND NINETEEN. THE SCHOOL WAS LOCATED NEAR WIMBLEDON COMMON, OUTSIDE OF LONDON. ELEANOR CAN BE SEEN IN THE BACK ROW, FIFTH FROM THE LEFT.

Often a teacher's pet is not popular with other students. Happily, this wasn't the case for Eleanor. Her fellow students admired her and valued her friendship. Having friends who enjoyed her company and looked up to her was something new for Eleanor, and she relished it. During her three years at Allenswood, Eleanor forged a new, more confident version of herself. Gone were the nervous headaches that had plagued her in New York. She no longer bit her fingernails to the quick. She would have loved nothing more than to stay at school for another year. Nevertheless, in 1902, Eleanor had to return home for a reason that she was dreading. It was time for the eighteen-year-old to make her debut in New York society.

The social season started in November, and young women

in the best families were expected to "come out" into society at fancy balls and exclusive dinners and luncheons. Eleanor's mother, Anna, had been the belle of her social season, and Eleanor was sure her debut would be unfavorably compared with her mother's success, which it was. It was also upsetting to know that the whole point of the season was to focus young women on finding suitable husbands.

Eleanor understood what Mlle. Souvestre meant when she had written to her student upon her return, "Protect yourself, my dear child . . . from . . . society's demands. There are more quiet and enviable joys than to be among the most sought-after women at a ball." Eleanor knew, however, she didn't have any choice in the matter.

The first dress ball she attended was "utter agony." But as the party-filled weeks went on, Eleanor began to feel more comfortable. Her sympathetic manner and intelligent conversation gave her some popularity, even if it was generally with the older crowd rather than her contemporaries. And although she still considered herself homely, she had a willowy figure and luminous blue eyes in her favor.

Eleanor had a lifelong frenemy (though no one knew that word then) in her cousin Alice, the eldest daughter of Theodore

Roosevelt, who was then president of the United States. As a child, Eleanor had been in awe of her confident cousin. Alice, pretty, brash, and outspoken, considered Eleanor a bit of a bore—but also a rival for her father's affections. Theodore Roosevelt cared deeply for his niece.

ELEANOR AND HER COUSIN ALICE, THE DAUGHTER OF PRESIDENT THEODORE ROOSEVELT, WERE TOTAL OPPOSITES: ELEANOR, RESPONSIBLE, SERIOUS, AND SHY; ALICE, BRAZEN AND CHATTY.

Alice also thought Eleanor's descriptions of herself were made to gain sympathy. "She was always making herself out to be an ugly duckling," Alice later observed about Eleanor during her cousin's debut year, "but she was really rather attractive." She added, "It's true that her chin went in a bit, which wouldn't have been so noticeable if only her hateful grandmother had fixed her [protruding] teeth."

It wasn't all parties and teas for Eleanor after her return to New York. She took on the responsibility of overseeing the boarding-school education of her bright eleven-year-old brother, Hall, whom she had showered with letters while she was abroad, and she took charge of the family's New York City town house, where she lived while her aunts and uncles flitted in and out.

Then Grandmother Hall decided the town house was too expensive to maintain, so she closed it up and moved to Tivoli. Elliott Roosevelt had run through most of his money before he died, so Eleanor only had a small inheritance to live on. Once more, she was at the mercy of relatives to take her in. Now it was her cousin and godmother, Mrs. Susie Parish, who gave her a place to live. The feeling that she never had a home of her own was something Eleanor struggled with well into adulthood.

Anxious to find a way to make her life more meaningful, Eleanor joined the Junior League. This was a newly formed organization of young socialites, like herself, who wanted to work on the many problems that faced the millions of immigrants who were flooding New York City. Jewish, Irish, Italian, they came to the United States fleeing danger and poverty or in search of a better life. They did find opportunity and freedom, but there was also uncertainty; crowded, unsanitary living conditions; and for those who found work—and that included children—endless hours of toil for low wages.

Eleanor wanted very much to help. But unlike many of the Junior League members who were content to hold fund-raising events, Eleanor was determined to be personally involved. She had never forgotten how, as a child, she had gone with an uncle to bring Christmas presents to children living in the worst part of the city, Hell's Kitchen. She had tagged along with her young aunts when they volunteered at a mission in another poor part of town, the Bowery. The Thanksgiving visit to the Newsboys' Lodge remained an outstanding memory of her father and a reminder that he often told her to grow up to be a woman he could be proud of. During the winter of 1903, Eleanor began volunteering at the settlement house on Rivington Street in New York's Lower East Side.

Settlement houses were like community centers where neigh-borhood residents

THE RIVINGTON STREET SETTLEMENT HOUSE WAS LOCATED ON NEW YORK CITY'S LOWER EAST SIDE, A PART OF TOWN OVERFLOWING WITH IMMIGRANTS WHO NEEDED HELP ADJUSTING TO THEIR NEW LIVES.

could go to takes classes to learn English and get help in practical pursuits like finding jobs and honing household skills. Young children were offered day care, and teaching little ones was where Eleanor found her niche, conducting classes in exercise and dance. Eleanor admitted that at first she didn't know what she was doing, but that didn't stop her from trying.

She also got to see firsthand, as one of her biographers put it, "misery and exploitation on a scale she had not dreamed possible." The people who came to the settlement house lived crammed together in tiny, dingy apartments called tenements. The bathroom facilities for these tenement dwellers were outdoors and shared by all the residents.

Sometimes Eleanor was frightened to be out on the dirty, dark streets of the Lower East Side, but she got great joy from the children she taught. When a father of one of her students gave Eleanor a small present because the child enjoyed her classes so much, Eleanor felt a "glow of pride."

But teaching wasn't the only way that Eleanor was involved with the immigrant community. While she was working at the Rivington Street Settlement House, a study was made of the working conditions of poor immigrant women and girls who earned money sewing garments in factories. The shocking report showed that working fourteen hours a day, six days a week for a wage of six dollars was not uncommon. Eleanor joined the National Consumers League, a group that wanted to change things, including by putting limits on child labor and pushing enforcement of the law allowing only a sixty-hour workweek.

Eleanor took on the job of inspecting these unsafe factories, called sweatshops, where women and girls labored over their sewing machines. "I was appalled . . ." she wrote in her autobiography. "I saw little children of four or five sitting at tables until they dropped with fatigue."

Something was stirring in Eleanor Roosevelt. The ideals of Mlle. Souvestre and Elliott's hopes for her were becoming realized in her work with the women and children of the immigrant community. Being useful, she found, was immensely satisfying.

But other feelings were stirring as well. Perhaps to her surprise, she had caught the fancy of a handsome young man, a distant cousin, and he wanted to marry her. She was only nineteen and he just a few years older, but that didn't matter, nor did the objections of his mother.

Eleanor was in love, and she could think of nothing more wonderful than becoming Mrs. Franklin Delano Roosevelt.

THE ENGAGED ELEANOR
AND FRANKLIN IN 1906

3

LOSING HERSELF

"Oh! Darling, I miss you so . . .
So very happy in your love dearest, that
all the world has changed for me . . ."

YOUR DEVOTED LITTLE NELL

Eleanor's signature in this 1904 letter to Franklin said as much as the loving words. Her father had called her Little Nell. Now she was sharing the cherished nickname with someone else who said he loved her.

How did Eleanor and Franklin get together? In some ways, they'd known each other practically all their lives. The large Roosevelt family tree had many branches. The couple were not only fifth cousins, but Eleanor's father, Elliott, was also Franklin's godfather—though he must have rarely seen him, since he didn't spend much time with his own children. Family lore recounted how Eleanor and Franklin had met on a visit when she was just two—the little boy gave her a piggyback ride. Over the years, they saw each other occasionally at family functions. Once, when she was fourteen and he sixteen, he asked the shy wallflower to dance at a party, a gesture that earned her gratitude.

Their relationship had its more serious beginning when they met by chance on a train in 1902, the summer before her debut into society. Franklin would start his junior year at Harvard in the fall. At Franklin's invitation, Eleanor rather nervously joined him and his formidable mother, Sara. Afterward, the young couple struck up a correspondence and then found reasons to be together—a lunch here, a dance there—though rarely unchaperoned. Well-brought-up young women were not supposed to be alone in the company of single men.

Soon the couple's feelings for each other began to grow. Being in the same social circles, they could be together at parties and balls, and Eleanor was also invited to parties at Franklin's family's summer home on Campobello Island in New Brunswick, Canada. Still, they tried to keep their budding relationship under wraps. It was in 1903, during a football weekend at Harvard, that the couple snuck away long enough for Franklin to propose.

Thousands, maybe millions, of words have been written about the relationship of Eleanor and Franklin Roosevelt and how different they seemed, at least on the surface. Certainly their childhoods had been almost polar opposites: Eleanor, an orphan, at the mercy of relatives, and without a home to call her own. Franklin, the cherished child of two devoted parents who gave him almost anything he wanted and doted on his every accomplishment. His growing-up years were idyllic, spent in the family home, Springwood, in Hyde Park, New York, on the banks of the Hudson River. He went swimming and boating in the summer, ice-skating in the winter, and all through the year enjoyed discovering the lush natural world that was right outside his window.

In personality and appearance the young couple seemed to be opposites as well. Where Eleanor was plain, shy, serious, and burdened with responsibilities before she was even a teenager, Franklin was handsome, outgoing, eternally optimistic, and carefree. One story has it that when Franklin proposed to her, Eleanor wondered aloud what he saw in her.

What he saw, as he put it even before they were courting, was a young woman with "a very good mind." As Franklin came to know Eleanor better, he was impressed with her intuitive and sympathetic nature. Perhaps inspired by his cousin Theodore, Franklin had big plans for his future, and he wanted a wife who was not just a pretty decoration but someone in whom he could confide. In answer to her question, he told her he was sure he could become something "with your help."

Despite the couple's differences, they held important values in common, and these were a bond. Franklin felt, perhaps not as deeply as Eleanor, but felt nonetheless, the importance of doing good. He would, on occasion, accompany her home after her classes at the Rivington Street Settlement House—an endeavor he supported—and his conscience was stirred by what he saw. Once, he went with her to take an ill student home and was shocked to see firsthand what tenement life was like. "My God," he said, "I didn't know people lived like that."

At Harvard, Franklin had written a paper about his family and their long history in America and concluded that their success came, in part, because of their sense of civic responsibility: "Having been born in a good position, there was no excuse for them if they did not do their duty by their community." His father, James, whom he much admired and who had died when Franklin was eighteen, had also urged him to think about his responsibilities to other people.

His mother, Sara, however, wanted him to think mostly about his responsibility to her. Sara Delano was twenty-six when she married James, who was then twice her age. Nevertheless, they were a congenial couple, and when Franklin was born, Sara felt her world was complete. She not only adored her only child, she wanted to keep him close; so much so that while other boys of his social class entered boarding school at twelve, she kept him home for another two years. When he started at Harvard, she took an apartment in Boston to be near him.

Having been around Sara and hearing the family gossip, Eleanor probably knew how tightly his mother tied Franklin to her apron strings. If not, Alice, with her sharp tongue, might have told her. She described him derisively as a "good little mother's boy." Eleanor probably wasn't even terribly surprised that after Franklin confessed to his mother that he'd proposed, Sara insisted they postpone the announcement, during which time Sara would take Franklin on a cruise.

ELEANOR'S WEDDING PORTRAIT.
SHE AND FRANKLIN WERE
MARRIED ON MARCH 17, 1905.

Although she didn't quite come out and say it, the purpose of the trip was to make Franklin forget about Eleanor.

Despite all of Sara's machinations, in the end she couldn't stop the wedding, which was to take place on March 17, 1905. Theodore Roosevelt had promised to give his niece away at her wedding, but since he was president, the event was hard to fit into his busy schedule. The date was chosen because he was going to be in New York for the St. Patrick's Day parade. After he was done marching, he would escort Eleanor down the aisle.

The wedding took place in a relative's home, a lavish affair with two hundred guests and six bridesmaids, including Alice. No one had considered that with the parade route so close to the wedding, the guests would have trouble reaching the house. Eleanor remembered years later, "A few irate guests arrived after the ceremony was over!" Those in attendance saw a stately Eleanor, dressed in satin and lace, carrying a lily of the valley bouquet, escorted down the aisle by her uncle, the president. Waiting at the altar was her handsome groom.

When the ceremony was over, President Roosevelt congratulated Franklin for keeping the name in the family and made a beeline for the refreshments. To Sara's indignation, the guests followed the witty, outspoken president and left the bride and groom standing alone. Eleanor shrugged it off. "I do not remember being particularly surprised at this," she recalled later. She and Franklin followed the laughter into the next room.

★

After a three-month honeymoon in Europe, Eleanor came home pregnant, and the first of their children, Anna, was born in 1906. After that, the babies came in rapid succession: James (1907); Franklin, Jr. (1909), who died at eight months old; Elliott (1910); another Franklin (1914); and finally John (1916).

Eleanor was uncomfortable with motherhood, and it showed. She veered from being too strict with her children to trying avant-garde methods of child-rearing—like rigging up a wire contraption to hold Anna outside a window after she read that fresh air was good for babies!

Without a real childhood of her own to use as a blueprint, she didn't know how to play with her children or be light-hearted around them, though sometimes she tried. Franklin, by contrast, with his big, boisterous personality, delighted in rolling around with his chicks, as he called them. But whether

ELEANOR AND FRANKLIN ON THEIR HONEYMOON IN SANREMO, ITALY

he was home or, as was often the case, busy with work, Eleanor was left to be the disciplinarian.

As adults her children described their mother as distant, dutiful, but unable to enjoy them. Eleanor, looking back, said that regretfully she didn't know anything about being a mother.

Sara took full advantage of this weakness. In many ways, often quite brazenly, Sara undermined Eleanor's mothering. She hired the help, who were loyal to her, won the children over with gifts and trips, and convinced herself she was more important to the children than their mother. She once told her grandson John, "Your mother only bore you. I am more your mother than your mother is."

Though her appropriation of the young Roosevelts may have been Sara's most outrageous action, it was at the top of a very long list of slights, insults, and overbearing behavior. The year Eleanor and Franklin married, Sara gave the young couple a Christmas gift—a drawing of a New York City town house that she was building for them. Actually, there were to be two town houses, one for them and one for Sara. The houses were connected by sliding doors through adjacent walls on three different levels.

Eleanor, afraid of displeasing Sara, went along with the decision to live so close together, but the house would remain a sticking point between them. Sara never stopped coming through those connecting doors. Eleanor remembered bitterly, "You were never quite sure when she would appear, day or night."

THE DRAWING OF THE TOWN HOUSE THAT SARA WAS HAVING BUILT FOR ELEANOR AND FRANKLIN. IT'S SIGNED, "FROM MAMA."

And where was Franklin in all this? Pretending as if the acrimony wasn't happening. Eleanor came to realize that no matter how much she longed for her husband's support, he wasn't going to take sides. He disliked unpleasantness and assumed eventually the two women would work things out.

Eleanor's unhappiness went on for years. Her frustrations and anger boiled into what she would call her "Griselda moods," named after a put-upon wife in Chaucer's *The Canterbury Tales*. The harder she tried to be the dutiful wife,

ELEANOR'S DISSATISFACTION WITH HER LIFE LEFT HER THIN AND UNHAPPY. EVEN AFTER SHE GAINED MORE CONTROL OVER HER LIFE, BOUTS OF DEPRESSION WOULD CONTINUE TO PLAGUE HER.

mother, and daughter-in-law, the more disagreeable—and depressed—Eleanor became.

Meanwhile, Franklin was forging ahead in his career. He had gone to Columbia Law School and supported his family while living in New York working at a law firm.

But being a lawyer didn't really suit the outgoing Franklin. He had higher ambitions, and the example of his cousin, President Theodore Roosevelt, showed him that politics might be a way to satisfy both his ego and his desire to be in public service.

In 1910, the Democratic Party asked him to run for the New York State Senate as a candidate from the Hyde Park area. Franklin was eager to take up the challenge, but the fact that he was a political novice showed. The first time Eleanor heard him make a speech, he spoke so slowly and his pauses were so long, "I worried for fear he'd never go on." Speaking style notwithstanding, he won, becoming the first Democrat to take the seat in thirty-two years. The town house was rented out and the family moved to Albany, the state capital. Eleanor hadn't been especially keen on Franklin getting into politics, but it did have one advantage: Sara didn't move with them. Nevertheless, she kept her presence felt with frequent visits.

Albany was a revelation for Eleanor. She thought politics

and government were going to be her husband's work. But as she soon learned, the politician's wife also had a role to play. Eleanor had to conquer her shyness and become Franklin's helpmate, hosting teas and luncheons and calling on the wives of allies and sometimes rivals. At first, for Eleanor this was just doing her wifely duty. As she put it, "Duty was perhaps the motivating force of my life . . . I looked at everything from the point of view of what I ought to do, rarely from the standpoint of what I wanted to do." But slowly, she became interested in what made government work and in the men—almost exclusively men—who pulled the political levers.

She looked for ways to be involved. She made social connections with government officials and their wives and figured out ways for Franklin to make political alliances, even with enemies. During Franklin's time in the state senate, Eleanor made it a practice to invite both sides of a political dispute to her home and make friends with everyone involved. "The first requisite of a politician's wife," she said, "is always to be able to manage anything." As one friend put it, "She was playing the political game far better than anyone else," but it was a game built on her real interest in people and her growing realization that the idea of championing the underdog was resurfacing as an important part of her life. As her success in political life grew, she began to build a strong base of political support for Franklin—and eventually for herself.

When it was time for Franklin to run for reelection, a man who would become an important influence on both Roosevelts stepped into their lives, Louis Howe. Howe saw a great future for Franklin Delano Roosevelt far beyond the New York State Senate. Howe became Franklin's closest adviser and helped him win his reelection race in 1912.

Initially, Eleanor, as she put it, "was not favorably impressed." A short, scrawny former newspaperman with a pockmarked face, a remnant of a serious childhood accident, Howe called himself one of the homeliest men in New York. And while

LOUIS HOWE, TRUSTED ADVISOR OF BOTH FRANKLIN AND ELEANOR, DRESSED CASUALLY AT HIS HOUSE ON HORSENECK BEACH IN MASSACHUSETTS

people did say he looked like a troll, it wasn't his looks that bothered Eleanor: It was his nonstop cigarette smoking that drove her crazy. He befouled the air and left ashes all over her house—and himself. It took a while for Eleanor to appreciate his political skill and personal devotion to the Roosevelts.

During the 1912 election, Franklin had campaigned hard not just for himself but for the Democratic candidate for president, Woodrow Wilson. Though loyally sticking with their party, this decision was awkward for Franklin and Eleanor because Theodore Roosevelt was running as a third-party candidate. Cousin Alice, though she remained friendly, especially with Franklin, never quite got over this betrayal.

Another family issue for Eleanor in 1912 was the marriage of her brother, Hall. Only twenty, he had been an excellent student at both his boarding school, Groton, and later at Harvard. Hall seemed to be making his way in the world, and his wife-to-be was a beauty. At the wedding, Eleanor said she "felt as if my own son and not my brother was being married." But despite his academic success, Eleanor was worried about her brother. It was clear that Hall was very much his father's son: He drank too much. She was right to be concerned. His drinking would get worse as the years went by.

It was only a few months after Franklin's reelection to the state senate that the new president, Wilson, rewarded his election loyalty by appointing him—at only thirty-one years old—assistant secretary of the navy. The job in the new administration was a huge step up from state politics, and, in fact, was the same job that had launched Theodore Roosevelt's political career culminating in the presidency. The secretary of the navy, Joseph Daniels, Franklin's boss, noted that fact in his diary with the hope, "May history repeat itself." Clearly some people were already seeing great things ahead for Franklin Delano Roosevelt.

While her husband got to work in March of 1913, Eleanor was left with the huge job of moving her family to Washington, D.C. Once again Eleanor was nervous about change, but building on the skills she'd learned in Albany, she learned her way around Washington and figured out how to navigate D.C. society's strict protocols. She also felt much more confident as a mother (and as in Albany, happy to be away from Sara's prying eyes). Franklin Jr. and John, who were born during this time in Washington, were raised by a much more relaxed mother.

Theodore Roosevelt, more forgiving than his daughter, was proud that Franklin held his old position in the navy. He recognized what others did—that Franklin, with his ability, wit, and charm, was a rising political star. In 1916, Woodrow

Wilson was reelected as World War I was raging in Europe. Wilson's position had been one of American neutrality, but when Germany sank American ships, the United States entered the war on April 6, 1917. Franklin's position at the navy now became even more important.

Once the United States was in the war, Eleanor noted, "the men in government worked from morning until late into the night. The women in Washington . . . began to organize . . . to meet the unusual demands of wartime." For Eleanor that meant volunteering at naval hospitals and at the Red Cross canteens, doing everything from making sandwiches (and once almost slicing off a finger while cutting bread) to supervising volunteers to washing floors. Getting out in the wider world— outside of politics—made her happy and broadened her per-spective. "I became a more tolerant person, far less sure of my own beliefs . . . I knew more about the human heart."

Eleanor had her hands full juggling the responsibility of children, her volunteer work, and the role of political hostess. She had servants to help run the house, but in 1914, she hired pretty twenty-two-year-old Lucy Mercer as her social secretary. Lucy, from a good but poor family, needed the work and did her job efficiently and with good humor.

Eleanor became very fond of Lucy, and so, as it turns out, did Franklin. Eleanor was not always in D.C., especially during the brutal, humid summers. She would take the children to stay with Sara at Springwood, or all of them would travel to Campobello Island.

The attraction between Franklin and Lucy grew, and they began a romance that flourished during Eleanor's absences. Some in Washington guessed about

LUCY MERCER, CIRCA 1915

the affair; others knew—including Alice, who took a certain amount of glee in dropping veiled hints to Eleanor. When Franklin canceled a trip to see the family on Campobello Island during the summer of 1917, Eleanor became suspicious.

In September 1918, the bottom dropped out of thirty-four-year-old Eleanor's world. Franklin came home after a work-related trip to Europe feeling unwell. Eleanor unpacked his bags. Tucked away, she found a packet of letters tied with a piece of velvet ribbon. As she read them, she

43

realized they were love letters from Lucy. The letters were the confirmation she'd been dreading. Eleanor immediately marched into Franklin's sickroom, letters in hand, and told him she would give him a divorce. Divorce was frowned upon at that time, but an angry Eleanor was ready to take that step.

Franklin may have wanted to marry Lucy, but reality intruded in the forms of Sara Roosevelt and Louis Howe, who'd moved to Washington to work for Franklin. Sara was furious. She told her son if he did something as scandalous as abandoning his wife and children, she'd snap her purse shut: Franklin would not have access to her considerable wealth. Louis, who believed that someday Franklin would be president, told him divorce and remarriage would mean his political career was over.

Franklin decided to stay in his marriage, and Eleanor agreed—with the stipulation he would never see Lucy again. Though the couple was going to stay together, Eleanor, shattered by the deception, was determined their life together would now be on a new footing. She appreciated Franklin's skill as a politician; she felt he had an important role to play in government and in the country. He was the father of her children, and she understood that in some way, she was going to have to continue in the role of his wife. But Franklin was no longer her great love, or if he was, she could no longer admit it.

Things were going to be different. Eleanor knew she would now have to decide what *she* wanted to do with her life—and then figure out a way to do it.

WITH NO MOTHER OF HER OWN, ELEANOR TRIED HARD TO FORGE A RELATIONSHIP WITH SARA. ALTHOUGH THERE WERE HAPPY MOMENTS AND TIMES OF AGREEMENT, ELEANOR FELT LIKE SHE WAS IN A DECADES-LONG TUG-OF-WAR WITH HER MOTHER-IN-LAW.

4

A LIFE TO BE LIVED

Once they decided to stay together, Franklin and Eleanor tried to mend the cracks in their marriage. Yet the deceit ate away at Eleanor, literally—she developed a form of anorexia. She also lost a good deal of the hard-won confidence she had worked for over the years. Still, she was ready to turn around her life. One defining moment came when she attended the funeral of Grandmother Hall at Tivoli in 1919. During the service, Eleanor pondered her grandmother's unhappy, unfulfilled existence. After being widowed, Mary Hall had done little with her life but try—unsuccessfully—to cope with her children. What a waste. Eleanor came away with one conclusion:

"Life was meant to be lived." And lived to the fullest on one's own terms.

FRANKLIN, SARA, ELEANOR, AND THE FIVE ROOSEVELT CHILDREN IN 1920

Eleanor set about making changes. For her own interest, she took typing and business classes. And she began taking charge of her household, to Sara's annoyance. In 1919, Eleanor dismissed all the white servants Sara had hired over the years and replaced them with black staff. Years later she wrote that perhaps it was "the Southern blood of my ancestors [who had owned slaves], but ever since I had been in

Washington, I had enjoyed my contact with such colored people as came to work for me. I never regretted the change which I made when I completely staffed my house with colored servants." This statement showed a naïveté about race relations, generally and personally.

Despite her previous interest in the plights of immigrants, Eleanor paid virtually no attention to the difficulties of African Americans, who faced prejudice every day. It would be almost two decades before she came to this understanding, despite her awareness of the great turmoil in the black community.

In 1919, while Franklin was serving as assistant secretary of the navy, terrible race riots rocked Washington, D.C. African American soldiers who thought fighting in World War I would open job opportunities or somehow decrease prejudice came home to even more segregation. As one historian put it, "The benefits of the war to make the world safe for democracy was restricted to whites."

The Ku Klux Klan was active, and not just in the South. Racial tensions spiked. In most cases, whites attacked blacks, and blacks fought back in more than thirty cities across the country during that hot summer. Washington, D.C., was one of them. Eleanor, who was at Campobello with the children, was worried about Franklin's safety, as her letters show: "No words from you and I'm getting anxious because of the riots. Do be careful not to be hit by stray bullets." The next day she added, "Still no letter or telegram from you and I'm worried to death."

Eleanor's and Franklin's concern in their continuous correspondence was for his personal safety. They didn't mention the riots in Washington, D.C., that left fifteen people, both white and black, dead, and many, many more injured. Nor did they discuss why the riot in Washington, D.C., was only one of dozens of race altercations across the United States that year. These riots and the lack of protection from law enforcement galvanized the African American community, and a new civil rights movement was born, though Eleanor and Franklin seemed oblivious to it.

Through much of Eleanor Roosevelt's adulthood, a thread emerged. She began to care for repressed communities when she came to know their members as individuals. As a young woman, she had casually made anti-Semitic comments; prejudice against Jews was common in her social circle. Her feelings changed when she made close friends who were Jewish. In 1919, she didn't know any African Americans except as servants. She may have felt sympathy for those who had been killed or wounded, as a general matter, but she had little interest in the root causes of black anger.

If the plight of African Americans was not a concern to Eleanor, there was one cause that caught her full attention after World War I. Eleanor became involved in the push for women's voting rights.

The fight to get women the right to vote in the United States had been going on since the 1850s. Women's suffrage had never been of much interest to Eleanor. She had always assumed men were "superior creatures" and could handle the voting. It was actually Franklin who became a suffragist first, in 1912. He was a state senator when a bill allowing women to vote in New York was presented to the legislature, and he backed it. Franklin's stance woke Eleanor up. It soon became apparent to her that the progressive reforms she was interested in seeing come about—better working conditions, child welfare laws, improved housing—would have more of a chance of happening if women could vote.

In 1920, the Nineteenth Amendment to the U.S. Constitution was ratified, and women were granted the right to vote (although some states had granted this previously). In less than three months, women were allowed to vote in a national election for the first time. Eleanor enthusiastically voted, and she also decided to get more involved by joining the League of Women Voters. The league's purpose was to inform women about issues and encourage them to get involved in the political process. Eleanor's talent for leadership was quickly recognized, and she was soon appointed to the league's board.

There was another important element to the 1920 presidential election for the Roosevelt family. Franklin, who had left his navy job to return to politics, was chosen to run for vice president on the Democratic ticket with presidential nominee James Cox. Once again, Eleanor was again asked to play the role of political wife, now following Franklin on the campaign trail. The long train trips around the country bored her at first. One of her chief jobs was motioning to her husband when he talked too long. His oratory had vastly improved since his first speeches, but he never spoke for five minutes when he could stretch it to ten.

Louis Howe saw more important work for Eleanor, however. Over the years, he had remained indispensable to Franklin, and Eleanor had come to appreciate his skills and overlook the cigarette ashes. Louis, for his part, had always been impressed by Eleanor's brains and instincts. He sought her input during the 1920 campaign, giving her early looks at Franklin's speeches and encouraging her to voice her opinions. He made sure to introduce her to both the politicians and newspaper reporters they met as they crossed the country, and she made friends in both groups. And perhaps just as important, he taught her how to speak in public effectively.

BEFORE TELEVISION, AND LONG BEFORE SOCIAL MEDIA, CANDIDATES FOR NATIONAL OFFICE CONDUCTED CAMPAIGNS BY RIDING TRAINS ACROSS THE COUNTRY, STOPPING IN CITIES AND TOWNS TO TALK TO VOTERS.

All Eleanor's insecurities came back in front of an audience. Her hands shook, her high voice could become screechy. Sometimes she would giggle from sheer nervousness. Louis, experienced in the ways of campaigns, worked with Eleanor and gave her simple rules she could follow that both calmed her and made her a much better speaker. His advice was: "Have something you want to say, say it, and sit down."

Almost everyone knew that the Cox-Roosevelt ticket didn't have much chance of winning, and it did lose to the Republican, Warren G. Harding, who became the twenty-ninth president. But during that campaign, Louis and Eleanor forged an unbreakable bond. Here was someone, Eleanor felt, who understood her and knew how to channel her energies. Louis was insistent in his belief that Franklin would be president of the United States and told Eleanor when Franklin's term was finished, he would make *her* president!

After Franklin's vice presidential loss, the family returned to their town house in New York City, and he to careers in both law and business. He hadn't made much money during his years in government and was eager to support his family without help from Sara.

For Eleanor, her confidence restored, the time had come to truly take back her life. Along with the League of Women Voters, she joined other progressive women's organizations dedicated to social change. Through this network, she made friends who broadened her horizons about everything from poetry to politics. These "New Women," as they were nicknamed, reminded Eleanor of Mlle. Souvestre and her ideas and ideals. Often unmarried or living with other women in same-sex relationships, members of Eleanor's circle were passionate about social reform and were not afraid to organize for political power. Eleanor felt comfortable with these bright and dedicated friends. They exemplified her goal of living life on one's own terms, and she was inspired by them. They were responsible, as she put it, "for the intensive education of Eleanor Roosevelt."

Then, in the summer of 1921, something happened that turned Eleanor's life upside down and threatened to dash every one of Franklin's political dreams.

It was August, and the Roosevelt family was on Campobello Island. They had spent a busy day sailing, swimming, even helping put

FRANKLIN AND ELEANOR ON CAMPOBELLO ISLAND. FRANKLIN'S PARENTS HAD HAD A HOME THERE SINCE 1883, AND IT BECAME A SUMMER HOME FOR ELEANOR AND FRANKLIN'S FAMILY. HERE THE COUPLE ENJOY THE BEACH IN 1920, THE SUMMER BEFORE HE CONTRACTED POLIO.

out a small fire on one of the neighboring islands. Franklin came down with a chill, and then he began running a fever. He went to bed, but the next morning he noticed his legs weren't working properly. Horrified, he soon realized that he was paralyzed from the waist down.

The local doctors were not able to make a diagnosis as Franklin's high fever grew worse. Finally, a specialist was brought up from New York. He gave the family the devastating news. Franklin had infantile paralysis—polio. Though the disease mostly struck children, adults were certainly not immune. Today, vaccination has wiped out polio in the United States, but in the 1920s, there was no cure and almost no treatment. It was a disease that frightened everyone, and the Roosevelts were no exception.

Eleanor sprang into action. She became Franklin's devoted nurse, exhausting herself. A doctor told her, "You will surely break down if you too do not get immediate relief." Eleanor did get assistance from the ever-present Louis Howe. Together, they took care of Franklin—bathing and massaging him, even brushing his teeth—until they could move him back to New York. Franklin, an optimist by nature, assumed that eventually he would fully recover, and Eleanor became his cheerleader.

It slowly dawned on all the Roosevelts that this wasn't to be. Over time, Franklin taught himself to shuffle his heavily braced legs forward for short periods, as long as he was holding on to someone's arm or on crutches, and to stand if gripping a lectern while giving a speech. But despite the appearance of movement, he never really walked by himself again. Although the public rarely saw it, Franklin spent most of his waking hours in a wheelchair.

Sara had been in Europe during the first few weeks of Franklin's illness. Upon her return, and as his prognosis became less hopeful, she argued—strongly—there was only one thing to do. Franklin must return to the place he'd loved since boyhood, Springwood in Hyde Park, and live quietly. Eleanor and Louis Howe were violently opposed to this notion of what his life should be. Louis still saw a great political future for him, while Eleanor knew that being idle and solitary was against everything in Franklin's outgoing nature.

One of Franklin's doctors, George Draper, witnessed "the intense and devastating influence of these high-voltage personalities on one another." A polio specialist, he found himself in the middle as Sara argued that her son should be treated as an invalid. Eleanor angrily replied that "if he fights he may overcome his handicap."

This was one battle Eleanor won and Sara lost. Dr. Draper told Eleanor she was right and that Franklin should live as normal and vigorous a life as possible. Though he'd spend the next several years recuperating, Franklin kept his hand in politics, staying active in both local New York happenings and on the national scene. In 1924, his rousing speech at the Democratic National Convention nominating Alfred E. Smith for president marked his full-time return to the political stage.

Once the dust of the medical crisis began settling, Eleanor and Franklin continued trying to find a way to lead their lives, apart and together. Franklin, in an effort to find relief and new treatments for his legs, began spending time first in Florida, then in Warm Springs, Georgia, where he eventually set up a sanitarium to help himself and other polio sufferers.

Eleanor did not care for the South—she didn't like the heat, the bugs, and the more casual lifestyle. Now approaching middle age, she spent most of her time in New York. She began to untangle herself from Sara—she even blocked the connecting doors to the town houses!—and took more responsibility for her children.

One stark realization was that Franklin could not be the same kind of father he was before his illness, especially to the younger boys, Franklin Jr. and John, who were only seven and five years old when their father contracted polio. The older children, Anna, James, and Elliott, had witnessed their father's physical agony as he'd tried to rehabilitate himself. They had been shocked, and Anna had become furious with her mother when she gave Anna's town house room to Louis during the first weeks after the family returned to New York from Campobello. But the three eldest could cope. "It began to dawn on me if the two youngest boys were going to have a normal existence," Eleanor wrote later, "I was going to have to become a good deal more companionable . . ." That she did, spending more time with them, and even taking the boys camping.

Even with all that was going on her life, Eleanor didn't slow down when it came to the causes that were ever more important to her. Her deep interest in politics and reform movements led her to become an ardent member of the New York State Democratic Committee. She edited the *Women's Democratic News*, a political newsletter, and perhaps most controversial, became a member of the Women's Trade Union League in 1922. This group, which some considered aligned with radicals, wanted women to form unions so they could insist on better working conditions. Eleanor not only raised money for the group, she also hosted parties for working-class women who, she felt, could use some fun in their lives.

ELEANOR ON CAMPOBELLO ISLAND IN 1925 WITH HER FRIENDS MARION DICKERMAN AND NANCY COOK

During the 1920s, Eleanor Roosevelt became a working woman as well. Along with her friend Marion Dickerman she bought the Todhunter School for upper-class girls in New York City, where she began teaching history and literature. It was a wonderful experience for Eleanor, who was able to emulate her heroine, Mlle. Souvestre, and in response received the same affection and respect from her own students. Decades later, one of those students stated emphatically, "And I never forgot a damned thing she ever taught me!"

Building on what she'd learned at Allenswood, Eleanor considered her main job was to get her students to think for themselves. It wasn't enough for them to regurgitate the lessons she taught. She demanded to know what *they* thought. In her literature courses, she made sure her students read women authors, and her educational goal was to lead her students "into an enlivened understanding of every possible phase of the world where they were going."

Still, as in many of her stands, there was contradiction. Though she believed wholeheartedly in public education (and that teachers, mostly women, were not paid enough), Todhunter was an expensive private school, the sort of place her own children went to.

In 1928, Franklin—often called by his initials FDR in newspaper headlines, a nickname that stuck—ran for and won the governorship of New York State, and Eleanor had to give up some of her own political work to take on the role of the state's First Lady. She still continued to take the train from Albany, the state capital, to Manhattan once a week to stay for several days of teaching. "I like teaching better than anything else I do."

It was a great source of pleasure to Eleanor that during his term, she and Franklin developed a serious working partnership. Since his mobility was limited, he often sent her out into the state to learn about the workings of various agencies and programs. One of her first visits was to a state hospital. When she returned, Franklin began asking her questions. "'What was the food like?' I said, 'Oh, I looked at the menus and they seemed very adequate.' And he said, 'I didn't ask you about the menus. I asked you what the food was like. You should have looked in the pots on the stove.' After that I was much better as an inspector."

One more thing happened during those years that made Eleanor's life easier and happier. She had never really felt comfortable at the Hyde Park estate. Springwood was Sara's house. Franklin came up with the idea to build a stone cottage on a piece of his land for Eleanor, Marion Dickerman, and their friend Nancy Cook (who was also a financial partner in Todhunter). The house, named Val-Kill after a nearby stream, was a sanctuary for Eleanor and where she lived when she was at Hyde Park. It was, at last, a home that she could call her own.

But there was another house calling—the White House. Eleanor knew that running for the presidency had always been

Franklin's long-term plan. It was not hers. Eleanor was content with the life she had and did not look forward to living in the White House fishbowl, where her every move would be watched and commented on. Nevertheless, in 1929 a national event occurred that rocked the United States to its core: The stock market

ELEANOR'S COTTAGE AT VAL-KILL WAS HER SANCTUARY FOR DECADES.

crashed, and the Great Depression began. People lost their savings and their jobs, and they watched the economy collapse. For a while, it looked as if the country might collapse as well, and the Republican president, Herbert Hoover, seemed unable to do much about it.

In 1932, Franklin ran for the presidency on the platform of a New Deal for Americans. If he won, he would have no less a job than repairing and restoring a broken country. Whatever her personal feelings, Eleanor knew she had to support the man she felt could handle that enormous job. And that man just happened to be her husband.

5

REACHING OUT

T he only thing we have to fear is fear itself!" This long-remembered line from Franklin Delano Roosevelt's inauguration speech in March of 1933 heartened the unemployed, impoverished, and worried citizens throughout the United States suffering through the third year of the Great Depression. But the new president knew that words would have to be followed by actions. After he took office, Franklin determinedly set out to get the country back on its feet.

The first one hundred days of Franklin's administration were a whirlwind of activity. They had to be, as the country was in crisis. A quarter of the workforce was out of work, more

FRANKLIN AND ELEANOR
RIDE TO HIS INAUGURATION
ON MARCH 4, 1933.

than a million people were homeless, banks were failing, and savings had disappeared. In those one hundred days, Franklin ignited his New Deal. He pushed fifteen major bills through Congress that attacked the Depression from all sides: banking, industrial changes, farm aid, employment, and social welfare. He spoke to the public in radio "fireside chats," and his calm and optimistic tone buoyed listeners across the country.

FRANKLIN DELIVERS HIS SIXTH FIRESIDE CHAT IN 1934.

Sometimes it seemed that the New Deal had formed an "alphabet soup" of agencies. There was the CCC, the Civilian Conservation Corps, providing jobs for young men in forestry and other conservation services; and the WPA,

THIS WELL WAS THE ONLY SOURCE OF WATER IN A TENNESSEE TOWN
UNTIL THE TENNESSEE VALLEY AUTHORITY HELPED MODERNIZE THE AREA.

the Works Progress Administration, employing millions to work on infrastructure projects like roads and bridges, while artists and writers and musicians carried out arts projects. The Tennessee Valley, a part of the country particularly hard-hit, was provided flood control and electricity by the TVA, the Tennessee Valley Authority.

The goal of these agencies and others was to provide direct relief to Americans. Some of the programs worked, others did not. A few, like one to regulate agricultural production, were ruled illegal by the courts. In 1935, Social Security was established, giving many older Americans a monthly stipend to help secure their futures. Though the Depression dragged on for years, finally ending with America's entry into World War II, the quick actions Franklin took did stabilize the country.

Eleanor, as always, did her duty. She had been correct about the fishbowl that was Washington, D.C. Everything she said, did, and even wore was scrutinized. Despite any personal discomfort, she soon realized that there was much she could do to help her country through this crisis, even though she had no formal title other than First Lady. But that was enough.

As he had done as governor of New York, Franklin used Eleanor as his eyes, ears, and legs. He started her traveling on a national scale, both to view actual conditions in the country and later to report on the progress his programs were making.

ELEANOR PUT HER STAMP ON THE ROLE OF FIRST LADY, TRAVELING THROUGHOUT THE COUNTRY—EVEN DOWN IN THE COAL MINES—AS AN ACTIVE PARTICIPANT OF HER HUSBAND'S ADMINISTRATION.

Sometimes she would go to the sites of federal relief projects unannounced, so she could see the real situations, not versions prettied up for the First Lady. It seemed Eleanor was everywhere: in rural areas, in crowded tenements, in national parks, in prisons, even down in a coal mine.

A problem arose when the head of the Secret Service discovered the independent First Lady was not going to allow an agent to accompany her on her travels. One day, he came to Louis and tossed a revolver on his desk and said, "Well, all right, if Mrs. Roosevelt is going to drive around the country alone, at least ask her to carry this in the car." In her autobiography, she reported, "I carried it religiously . . . I asked a friend, a man who had been one of Franklin's

ELEANOR LEARNS HOW TO SHOOT A GUN.

bodyguards in New York State, to give me some practice in target shooting so that if the need arose I would know how to use the gun." It took a good deal of practice, but Eleanor did become knowledgeable about handling guns.

★

Republicans, who didn't like the Roosevelts and their activism, along with some members of the press, made fun of Eleanor and her travels. (A newspaper published a half-joking prayer, "Just for one day, God, please make her tired.") But most Americans admired her efforts. They began to feel she was a friend and started writing her letters. Before bed, after long days that might include a visit to a CCC camp or hosting a dinner for foreign dignitaries—or both!—she would try to answer her mail. "From March 1933 to the end of the year, I received three hundred one thousand pieces of mail . . . ," she reported. "The variety of the requests and apparent confidence that I would be able to make almost anything possible worried me."

Though she could not, of course, answer most personally, she did reply to a cross section, referred others to the proper government agencies, and sometimes offered advice or even money to those who sounded desperate.

She also continued a practice she had started during the 1920s, getting paid for writing books and newspaper columns and guesting on radio programs. A First Lady receiving wages was unheard of, and though Eleanor did receive criticism about this, especially from Republicans, her writing proved extremely popular—and profitable. The money allowed her to continue giving money to the charities of her choice.

Through her travels and writings, Eleanor was in touch with everyday people and seemed to have her finger on the pulse of the country. She continued to be particularly interested in women's issues, while a new focus was the youth of America. She was concerned that the United States was in danger of losing a whole generations of young Americans—"a stranded generation," she called them—disillusioned with an economic system that had let them down and left them with little hope for the future.

ELEANOR AT SHE-SHE-SHE CAMP FOR UNEMPLOYED WOMEN IN BEAR MOUNTAIN, NEW YORK. THE FIRST LADY WAS THE DRIVING FORCE BEHIND THE CAMPS. THE CIVILIAN CONSERVATION CORPS WAS DESIGNED FOR YOUNG MEN ONLY, WHOSE WORK INVOLVED FORESTRY AND UTILIZING THE COUNTRY'S NATURAL RESOURCES. ELEANOR MADE SURE THERE WERE PROGRAMS FOR JOBLESS WOMEN AS WELL.

It was Eleanor's determination and persistence in lobbying her husband, as well as others in the administration, that led to the formation of another successful entry in the alphabet soup of commissions: the NYA, the National Youth Administration, or as Franklin affectionately called it, "the missus organization." NYA programs gave grants to high school and college students to help them stay in school, and those who had dropped out could apply for job-training programs. Using a similar "family" metaphor, the head of the program in North Carolina echoed a sentiment heard around the country in a letter to Eleanor. "Out here we think of the NYA as your government child. Certainly no member of the alphabet family is more popular."

Despite her history as a politically astute reformer and champion of the underdog, there continued to be one group that didn't receive much of Eleanor's attention. She was in her forties and First Lady of the United States before she began to seriously look at the problem of racism in America and the injustices faced by its African American (then called Negro or colored) citizens. But once she did, she was determined to help.

Why was racism still such an issue almost seventy years after the end of the Civil War in 1865? The Thirteenth Amendment to the Constitution, ratified in December 1865, ended slavery. The Fourteenth Amendment, ratified in 1868, gave former slaves citizenship and all persons born in the United States equal protection under the law. The Fifteenth Amendment, ratified in 1870, said that race could not be used as a reason to deny the right to vote—for men only, of course; women wouldn't get the vote for another fifty years.

Northern troops occupied the South until 1877, a period called Reconstruction, and enforced these laws. One of the results was that African American men were elected to public office. Another result was the simmering anger of many white citizens who had lost not only the war, but their way of life. When the troops left the South, ways were found to disenfranchise black voters and return political and economic power to whites.

A system of strict segregation was set up in which blacks were kept separate socially from whites and in subservient positions. African Americans in the Southern states had to defer to white people, eat in their own establishments, go to their own schools, sit separately in public venues, use public bathrooms for blacks only, and even drink from their own water fountains.

Other parts of the United States had their own forms of segregation. Some were codified into law, for instance, the separation of blacks and whites in hotels and a prohibition on intermarriage; other restrictions were more a matter of custom than regulation. These laws varied in different Northern and Western states. In the South, they were more uniform and harsher, and the penalties for breaking them often more severe. These were called Jim Crow laws, named for a stage character insulting to blacks.

During the hard times of the Depression, there wasn't much for whites or blacks, but African Americans always got the shorter end of the stick. Nevertheless, there were groups fighting hard for change against sometimes dangerous, always overwhelming odds. The best known was the NAACP, the National Association for the Advancement of Colored People. Founded in 1909, its goals included political, educational, social, and economic equality under the law.

With her sensitivity to people, especially those whose lives were difficult through no fault of their own, it would seem Eleanor should have been an early supporter of African American rights and groups like the NAACP. So why wasn't she?

As with many people, her racism began in childhood. Eleanor's paternal grandmother, Martha Bulloch Roosevelt, was raised in the South before the Civil War, where she had lived on a plantation. Though Martha had died a few months after Eleanor's birth, the girl grew up hearing romanticized stories from her great-aunt Annie, Martha's sister, about the Bulloch girls' happy childhood in Georgia. As a part of plantation life, the sisters had young slaves, called shadows, who waited on the girls and slept at the foot of their beds. As a girl, Eleanor enjoyed the tales. She never thought about the stories from the enslaved children's points of view.

But even as an adult, she didn't consider African American sensitivities. One of her biographers has speculated that approaching middle age, the only blacks she knew were servants. Her road to racial sensitivity was not only slow but uneven. As late as 1936, even after her ideas about social justice had begun to broaden, she could be thoughtless. One example—she was still using the offensive term *darky*, and in her autobiography, no less.

Eleanor was put on the defensive by a young African American woman, a graduate of Tuskegee University, who saw the word *darky* while reading a magazine excerpt of Eleanor's autobiography. She wrote to the First Lady: "I couldn't believe my eyes" when I came across the "hated" and "humiliating" term. The writer continued that it was even more shocking having been written by a women she admired so much.

Eleanor responded, "*Darky* was used by my Georgia great aunt as a term of affection, and I have always considered it in that light. I am sorry if I hurt you." A chastised Eleanor asked, "What do you prefer?"

VISITING NEW DEAL PROGRAMS TO SEE HOW THEY WERE WORKING WAS AN IMPORTANT PART OF HOW ELEANOR SAW HER JOB AS FIRST LADY. HERE SHE IS VISITING A WPA AFRICAN AMERICAN NURSERY SCHOOL ON DES MOINES AVENUE IN IOWA IN 1936. MANY OF THE NEW DEAL PROGRAMS IN BOTH THE NORTH AND SOUTH WERE SEGREGATED.

The awakening of Eleanor's social consciousness had begun with her charity visits as a child and working at the Rivington Street Settlement House as a young adult. Later, issues like child labor and workers' rights captured her attention and energy. But for many years, she only saw herself doing good works from a position higher than those she was helping. She didn't consider them as equals.

It was over the course of her adulthood, especially after she became First Lady, as she traveled and talked, observed and learned, that Eleanor began seeing the common humanity she shared with people of all races. As one historian put it, "She was not afraid to allow herself to change and become a better, more accepting, more balanced and informed person."

This was perhaps most true when it came to her willingness to stand by the side of those fighting for their civil rights. Her personal friendships with individuals of color finally brought Eleanor to a greater understanding of what African Americans endured, and in many ways this shocked her. The White House was to become her new schoolhouse, the place where she would truly begin to learn what it meant to be black in America.

6

A NEW STANDARD FOR UNDERSTANDING

A very different Eleanor Roosevelt came to Washington, D.C., in 1933 than the one who had lived there when her husband was the assistant secretary of the navy during World War I, almost twenty years before. This Eleanor realistically understood her shortcomings, but she had also developed many strengths. Two of the most important were her ability to spot inequalities and a willingness to do something about them.

One of the first things she did after her husband's inauguration was to visit the slums of Washington, D.C. The crusade to dismantle the filthy alley slums of D.C., home to mostly African Americans, had been led by another First Lady, Ellen

Wilson, the first wife of President Woodrow Wilson. The housing, constructed in hidden alleys behind the stately homes and public buildings of Washington, had long been declared a health hazard because the horrendous conditions there bred disease.

Eleanor, during her first stay in Washington, knew of Mrs. Wilson's efforts but hadn't done much to support them. Now, the new First Lady learned that things had not changed since Mrs. Wilson died in 1914. (On her deathbed, Ellen Wilson was told a law had been passed that would clear the slums, but World War I intervened and nothing was done.)

On a blustery March day in 1933, Eleanor, in one of her first acts as First Lady, toured the alley slums. Accompanied by a longtime crusader for better housing, Charlotte Everett Hopkins, who had urged the visit, she was driven through a small crevice opening into a rotten world of crumbling wooden tenements, home to twelve thousand blacks and one thousand whites. There was no running water and only outdoor bathrooms. The rarely collected garbage was a magnet for well-fed rats that darted everywhere.

Eleanor didn't just look on this visit, she listened. The residents described the horrors of life in the dirty tenements,

the indignities, the disease, the desperation. These shocking sights and conversations convinced the First Lady to
take on the crusade of decent housing. She talked about it,
wrote about it, and a year later she spoke at the first National
Housing Conference, calling out slumlords as "thoughtless
people" who would force others to live in squalid conditions
"just to make a little more money." She took her post of hon-
orary chairman of the Washington Committee on Housing
seriously, helping to pass legislation that created the Alley
Dwelling Authority of 1934, which tore down and rebuilt or
renovated the inadequate housing.

Eleanor's concern with decent housing led to one of her
pet projects, a planned community in West Virginia called
Arthurdale. The Appalachia area was one of the poorest in a
country that was almost drowning in poverty. Lorena Hickok,
Eleanor's close friend and a newspaper reporter now working
for the Roosevelt administration, had been sent to inspect
conditions in various parts of the United States. The worst
she had seen was a coal mining area called Scott's Run in West
Virginia. The name "Run" came from the stinking waste that
trickled down the side of the hills. Hickok reported, "Along the
main street through the town, there was stagnant, filthy water,

which the inhabitants used for drinking, cooking, washing, and everything else imaginable."

A COAL MINING FAMILY IN WEST VIRGINIA

Eleanor came to see for herself. She met a community of starving people who talked to her about what it was like to live in abject poverty. Despite different settings, the problems of poor people in rural West Virginia and urban Washington, D.C., were very similar.

In one shack she saw a little boy who held a white rabbit close in his arms, obviously his pet. Eleanor recounted how his sister told her, "He thinks we are not going to eat his rabbit.

But we are." Hearing that, the boy fled down the hill, still clutching the rabbit to his chest.

Eleanor used this story to help raise money for the new community of Arthurdale. What began as an idea to move out-of-work coal miners to West Virginia farmland became a planned community, where the residents could farm as well as work in light industries. Franklin got behind the program, and Congress approved twenty-five million dollars for the project, with hopes it might possibly serve as a prototype for other such communities. Still, there were critics aplenty who disapproved of why and how so much money was being spent.

ELEANOR MEETS WITH THE RESIDENTS OF THE NEW ARTHURDALE COMMUNITY IN 1935.

The first prefabricated homes in Arthurdale were ready for occupancy in 1934. Thanks in part to Eleanor's fundraising efforts among her wealthy friends, Arthurdale became a true community, with a clinic and good schools. She used her connections to bring a furniture factory and a vacuum cleaner assembly plant to the area.

In the end individual families benefited from Arthurdale, but the area as a whole did not. Congress turned against the project, finding it too expensive to continue financing. By 1941, Eleanor herself conceded that money had been wasted, but, she thought, money had also been saved: "I have always felt that many human beings who might have cost us thousands of dollars in tuberculosis sanitariums, insane asylums, and jails were restored to usefulness and given confidence in themselves."

There was one aspect of the Arthurdale experience, however, that shocked her. Even though whites and blacks had been living together in poverty in the region for decades, white residents of Arthurdale refused to allow African Americans to join them in their new community. Six hundred families, including two hundred black families, originally applied for housing, but the first fifty families, chosen by a committee from the University of West Virginia, were all white.

These first families formed the Arthurdale Homesteaders Club, which was allowed to make its own rules for their community. The First Lady requested that the next group of residents be more diverse, but the Homesteaders Club refused, writing her that they were "thoroughly opposed to Negroes as residents, and we feel that we should not risk the loss of respect we have gained in the community by admitting Negroes." They also made the point that the community would need separate schools, since West Virginia law forbade integrated schools.

This was an eye-opening turn of events for Eleanor. She was now starting to understand just how corrosive the systematic segregation of African Americans was. Unlike many Americans, even liberals and progressives who preferred not to look at the problem, she saw racism for what it was: a disease to the body of the United States that needed to be examined and cured.

To that end, Eleanor began to surround herself with people who were already working on the cause of civil rights, though that name had yet to be commonly given to the movement. One of those people was a woman she had met in 1927, an African American educator named Mary Jane McLeod Bethune.

ELEANOR CAME TO REGARD MARY JANE MCLEOD BETHUNE AS ONE OF HER CLOSEST FRIENDS.

Mary was the fifteenth of seventeen children born to a pair of former slaves in South Carolina. The only child in her family to attend her local one-room schoolhouse, she'd come home, after walking five miles back and forth, to teach her family what she'd learned each day. Her teacher helped her get scholarships to continue her learning. As an adult, she dedicated herself to education and starting schools for blacks.

Now married to another educator, Mary first encountered Eleanor at a meeting of the National Council of Women in 1927. She was the last to arrive in a room filled with white women, and she wasn't sure where she should sit. Later she remembered how Sara Roosevelt got up from her seat, took her arm, and led her to a chair between her and Eleanor. "I can remember, too, how the faces of the Negro servants lit up with pride when they saw me seated at the center of that imposing gathering." Whatever Sara's other faults, she was not a racist, mostly because her father, an educator, taught tolerance rather than prejudice. This encounter over time led to a fast friendship between the Roosevelt women and Mary Jane McLeod Bethune.

Another person who came into the First Lady's orbit was Walter Francis White, the head of the the NAACP. Walter, of mixed European and African heritage, had blue eyes and light hair and could easily have passed for white. Instead, he spent his life fighting injustice against African Americans.

Walter was among a small group of notable black leaders and educators who were invited by Eleanor to a dinner meeting at the White House in January 1934. She wanted it known that the Roosevelt administration was interested in their concerns. For over four hours in a no-holds-barred conversation, the participants discussed and debated the problems facing their race. As one historian put it, "Never before had black leaders been invited to discuss unemployment, lynching, unequal expenditures to educate children, and the failure to provide housing, sanitation, and running water."

The group decided that as much as they would like to tackle the huge issue of segregation, there was a more immediate problem to focus on—making sure that blacks got their fair share of the New Deal programs, which at the moment was not happening.

Franklin was wheeled in after midnight to say hello to the group and offer his support. But in the coming years, it would be Eleanor, not Franklin, who kept the issue of civil rights front and center in the Roosevelt administration. As one participant in that unprecedented evening meeting put it, Eleanor "set before all of us a new standard for understanding and cooperation in the field of race."

There was one more person who came along a few years later and helped the First Lady open her eyes. She was one of Eleanor's many correspondents, a young African American woman named Pauli Murray.

Pauli first saw Eleanor in 1933, when the First Lady was visiting a camp for unemployed women in upstate New York. Shy and nervous about meeting the president's wife, she

A YOUNG PAULI MURRAY, WHO WOULD
BECOME A LIFELONG FRIEND

hid behind a book she was reading. After the visit, Pauli was called out by the camp's director for her disrespect. When she wrote to Eleanor in 1938, she used this incident to remind the First Lady that she was "the girl who did not stand up" at Camp Tera.

Her note to Eleanor was attached to a copy of a letter she'd sent to President Roosevelt about being denied admission to her state school, the University of North Carolina, because of her race. In it, she wrote with eloquence, passion, and sadness about what it felt like to be black in America. "Twelve millions of your citizens have to endure insults, injustice, and such degradation of spirit that you believe impossible as a human being . . . Can you, for one moment, put yourself in our place and imagine the feelings of resentment, the protest, the indignation, the outrage that would rise within you to realize that you, a human being, with the keen sensitivities of other human beings, were being set off in a corner, marked apart from your fellow human beings?"

Pauli, who had copied Eleanor because she thought there was better chance of the First Lady reading the letter than her husband, closed by noting that segregation "isn't my problem alone, it is the problem of my people, and in these trying days, it will not let me or any other thinking Negro rest."

This letter, the first in series of letters between the two women that would last until the end of Eleanor's life, was yet another thread in the tapestry of anger and despair that she now saw as the plight of African Americans. As the First Lady of the United States, she decided to use her position to work side by side with black leaders who were leading the charge for their equal rights.

Eleanor Roosevelt now firmly believed that by making the country a better place for its African American citizens, it would become a better place for all its citizens.

7

THE SPUR

Eleanor thought it was important to show African Americans they had a friend in the White House. Though the struggle was theirs, it was useful to have a backer who had the president's ear. She kept her eye on New Deal legislation to make sure laws were evenly applied to both blacks and whites. She also tried to use her influence to make sure African Americans were placed in significant positions in New Deal agencies. Neither of these issues was always met with success.

There was one civil rights fight, however, that had particular urgency. It pitted Eleanor against Franklin, beginning in his first term in office and continuing throughout his presidency. It concerned a despicable American tradition: lynching.

Lynching was the hanging (sometimes with burning, torture, and dismemberment) of usually minority men, women, and young people by mobs. Lynchings were all too familiar after the Civil War and through the years

CROWDS GATHER IN WACO, TEXAS, TO WATCH THE 1916 LYNCHING OF JESSE WASHINGTON.

leading into World War II. One of the most horrifying things about public lynchings was that they were often festive public spectacles, with both adults and children in the audience. One newspaper called them "carnivals of death." Sometimes postcards were sold as souvenirs of the events.

Although about 85 percent of victims during this time period were blacks and the lynchings happened mostly in Southern states, other minorities, such as Mexicans and Chinese Americans—as well as whites—were also targeted, and states including Minnesota, California, and New York were places where lynchings occurred.

The NAACP, among other organizations, was anxious to have a federal law passed against lynching, and two senators, Robert F. Wagner of New York and Edward P. Costigan of Colorado, proposed a bill to make lynching a federal crime. Eleanor was a staunch backer of the law, and tried to get Franklin to put his considerable presidential weight behind its passage. But this turned out to be impossible.

It wasn't that Franklin didn't believe in the merits of the bill. He did. He had spoken out about lynching in one of his radio fireside chats on December 6, 1933, saying, "We know that it is murder . . . We do not excuse those in high places or low who condone lynch law." But the Costigan-Wagner Bill posed a huge political problem for him. The Senate was controlled by Democratic senators from the South. If Franklin came out too strongly for the anti-lynching bill, he would anger those senators who felt the federal government had no right to interfere in what they considered issues of states' rights.

It's hard to understand how the murder of people in the most brutal way possible would be something that lawmakers could disagree about. But since the Civil War, the Southern states were hypersensitive to federal interference. It was also true that since Reconstruction, the Southern states were looking for ways to take away rights, including voting rights of African Americans. To that end, Southern state governments disenfranchised voters by charging poll taxes and administering literacy tests. When that didn't work, there was always intimidation.

African Americans who were lynched were often not accused of any real crimes but rather of behavior considered impudent or inappropriate by the social structure, for instance, a black male whistling at a white woman or a person of color not acting with enough deference to whites. Sometimes the charges were made up or used to take property from African Americans. Lynching frightened people and kept them in their place.

In 1933, there were twenty-eight lynchings; twenty-four of the victims were black. Walter White of the NAACP continuously discussed with the First Lady the progress of the Costigan-Wagner Bill and asked her to press the president for his support. She tried, but in May of 1934, she wrote White a letter saying, "The President talked to me rather at length today about the lynching bill. As I do not think you will either like or agree with everything that he thinks, I would like an opportunity of telling you about it . . ." She also offered to set up a meeting with the president.

Franklin was famous for using his charming personality and telling amusing anecdotes to defuse uncomfortable situations. That's what he tried to do when he joined Eleanor and his mother, Sara, during a meeting they had set up with Walter White on May 7, 1934. Franklin tried to explain why politics made it impossible to support the bill. Walter argued with him. The president became frustrated.

He turned to his wife. Had she coached Mr. White? Franklin asked. Eleanor mildly suggested they continue talking. Then the president turned to his mother, "Well, at least I know you'll be on my side." Sara "shook her head." No, she was on Walter's side.

Franklin threw up his hands. Finally, he firmly explained the political realities to Walter: "I did not choose the tools with which I must work. But I've got to get legislation passed by Congress to save America. . . . The Southerners, by reason of the seniority rule [in Congress], are chairmen or occupy strategic places on most of the Senate and House committees. If I come out for the anti-lynching bill now, they will block every bill I ask Congress to pass to keep America from collapsing. I just can't take the risk."

Walter White did get Franklin's assurance that if the

bill came to his desk he would sign it. But the bill was never passed.

In October of 1934, a black man, Claude Neal, accused of murdering a white woman, was taken from a jail in Alabama and moved back to Florida, where the crime had been committed. Neal's captors were so bold, the lynching was advertised in advance, so people could come out to watch. News of the lynching spread across the country through newspapers and radio. Soon the Florida governor was receiving telegrams telling him to stop this tragedy in the making, but he and other local authorities did nothing. The crowd that came to watch numbered perhaps in the thousands, and those holding Neal, fearful of a riot, decided to lynch him in private. But first they tortured him in horrible ways, including cutting off parts of his body.

After the deed was done, the waiting crowd demanded the body and inflicted more damage. The mob's anger spilled over, and people began burning whatever property they could find in the area that belonged to blacks. It took the arrival of the National Guard to quell the anger.

This horrifying event galvanized the black community and its supporters. In fact, this disgusting episode disturbed people all across the United States, and support for the anti-lynching bill grew.

A protest meeting at New York City's Carnegie Hall was planned, and Walter White wanted the First Lady to speak. She informed Franklin about the meeting and told him she was inclined to take part, but said she would do whatever he thought best. The president told her that to make that speech would be political "dynamite." Eleanor apologized to Walter and stayed away.

THE RELATIONSHIP BETWEEN ELEANOR AND FRANKLIN WAS A COMPLICATED ONE, BUT THEY ALWAYS RESPECTED EACH OTHER AND DID THEIR BEST TO SUPPORT ONE ANOTHER, SOMETIMES WITH VARYING DEGREES OF SUCCESS.

Franklin admired his wife and rarely told her not to do something. Eleanor had once asked Franklin if he minded her speaking out. "No, certainly not," he answered genially. "You can say anything you want. I can always say, 'Well, that's my wife, I can't do anything about her.'"

Yet he could also make it clear, as with the dynamite comment, when something was not in the best interest of him or his administration. One of Eleanor's roles, as she saw it, was to be her husband's conscience. She had a way of looking at him and saying, "Now, Franklin . . ." or leaving notes and articles for him. She expected him to learn about and hopefully act on the issues she brought to him. Yet she also understood—and often told those who wanted her support on a range of issues—that Franklin was the president, not she. He was the only one to make the ultimate decisions on matters of state.

During the early spring of 1935, the Costigan-Wagner Bill was brought to the Senate floor. The Southern senators prepared to filibuster the bill. That meant this bloc would hold the floor and make sure no other legislation could pass until the anti-lynching bill was killed. Franklin, who continued to need his New Deal legislation passed, would not say anything against the filibuster, which went on for several weeks before the sponsors of the bill agreed to withdraw it. Eleanor wrote to a disappointed Walter, "Of course, we will all go on fighting."

The anti-lynching bill was debated again in 1937; Republicans in Congress supported the bill, and the House passed it, moving it along to the Senate. Eleanor implored her husband to support the bill, but the president once again insisted he needed the Southern Democratic senators for help with his other legislation. There was another filibuster. This time, during the long days of talking, the First Lady watched from the Senate gallery "in silent rebuke of the shameful tactic." The bill died in the Senate later that fall. Other attempts were made to pass anti-lynching legislation during Franklin's terms in office, but all met the same fate.

There were efforts to pass an anti-lynching bill in succeeding years. All failed until 1946, after Franklin's terms had ended.

The failures of the anti-lynching bills were deeply disappointing, but Eleanor continued to push her husband for more support on the overall issue of civil rights. Louis Howe, her ally and supporter, had died in 1936, but she found several strong supporters in the administration, including Harold Ickes, the secretary of the interior, and presidential adviser Aubrey Williams, who called himself a Southern rebel because though he was from the South, he championed African Americans' rights. Many other members of the president's inner circle, however, disliked Eleanor's outspoken views on race relations and resented the way she tried to push her agenda with him.

Eleanor never in doubted that Franklin respected her views and appreciated her efforts. It was also clear her husband often found her to be relentless and even annoying at times when it came to her pursuit of causes she believed in. She once noted, perhaps sadly, "He might have been happier with a wife who was completely uncritical. . . . Nevertheless, I think I sometimes acted as a spur, even though the spurring was not always wanted or welcome. I was one of those who served his purposes."

IT NEVER HURTS TO BE KIND

President Roosevelt won reelection for a second term in 1936 in a landslide, losing only two states. One element in his sweeping win was the support of the African American community. Traditionally, African Americans had voted for the Republican Party, the party of Abraham Lincoln, who had freed the slaves. Herbert Hoover had received the majority of their votes in the 1932 election, but the New Deal legislation of the Roosevelt administration, as well as Eleanor's personal advocacy for African American concerns, was swinging their votes to the Democrats.

With four more years of a Roosevelt administration ahead of her, Eleanor was again ready to use her position as First

Lady to advance the cause of civil rights in ways large and small.

Moving a chair might not seem like a big deal, but it was in 1938, when Eleanor was attending the Southern Conference for Human Welfare in Birmingham, Alabama. On the first day of the large gathering, white and black attendees had mixed freely. When the police commissioner, Eugene "Bull" Connor—later to become infamous for his cruel treatment of civil rights protesters—got wind of this, he sent police to the auditorium the next day to make sure segregation laws were enforced.

The police arrived at municipal auditorium and told the participants they had to segregate themselves according to race. Eleanor, who had taken a seat next to her friend, Mary Jane McLeod Bethune, was informed personally that she needed to get up and move to the white section. The First Lady had her own solution to the problem. She picked up her chair and placed it in the center aisle, on neither the black nor the white side of the room. And there she sat for the rest of the program.

At Eleanor's suggestion, Mary had already been appointed to an important post in the Roosevelt administration. She was named director of Negro Affairs for the National Youth Administration, where she successfully oversaw programs that helped tens of thousands of young black people find jobs or be accepted in job training programs. The governmental appointment didn't stop Mary's other civil rights activities, and because she was friends with the First Lady, her concerns got a fair hearing at the White House.

There was, however, something about the relationship between the two women that bothered Eleanor. It was her habit to give her women friends a friendly peck on the cheek when she greeted them. Yet she didn't kiss Mary, and she knew it was because she didn't feel comfortable kissing a black person. One day, without thinking about it, she kissed her. Eleanor's daughter, Anna, reported years later that this kiss was a personal milestone for her mother.

Another prominent African American woman was affected by the actions of the First Lady. The opera singer Marian Anderson was known around the world for her magnificent contralto voice. She had already sung for a small group at the White House. But in 1939, Anderson's manager wanted to hold a concert in Washington, D.C. The only venue large enough to hold the anticipated crowd was Constitution

Hall, which was owned by the Daughters of the American Revolution (DAR), a group of white women descended from those who fought in the Revolutionary War or aided in gaining independence from Britain. The organization informed Anderson's manager that Constitution Hall was "not available to Negro artists."

Marian Anderson said she was "shocked beyond words to be barred from the capital of my own country after having appeared in almost every other capital of the world."

Eleanor was a member of the DAR, and she was disgusted when she learned that the group had refused to let a black artist, and a distinguished one at that, perform at Constitution Hall. She resigned from the organization, writing in her letter, "You had an opportunity to lead in an enlightened way, and it seems to me that your organization failed."

Both Eleanor and Franklin encouraged the secretary of the interior, Harold Ickes, to arrange for an outdoor concert for Anderson on the steps of the majestic Lincoln Memorial. Then, the First Lady used her contacts in radio to have the concert broadcast across the country. On April 13, 1939, Secretary Ickes introduced Marian Anderson with the words, "Genius knows no color line."

ELEANOR'S ROLE IN HAVING MARIAN ANDERSON SING AT THE LINCOLN MEMORIAL INCLUDED HER SUGGESTION THAT THE NAACP USE THE RADIO BROADCAST OF THE EVENT TO RAISE MONEY FOR THEIR ORGANIZATION. HERE SHE MEETS WITH THE SINGER IN JAPAN IN 1953.

With the statue of Abraham Lincoln behind her, the singer began her concert with "My Country, 'Tis of Thee" and ended it with the Negro spiritual, "Nobody Knows the Trouble I've Seen." Seventy-five thousand people, black and white, turned out that Easter Sunday to hear Marian Anderson sing.

Eleanor's outreach to African Americans did not go unnoticed, especially when they were invited guests to the White House, a place built with slave labor. Notable African Americans had visited the White House before. Abraham Lincoln had met with abolitionists Frederick Douglass and Sojourner Truth there during the Civil War. Educator and author Booker T.

Washington was the first African American to be invited for dinner then, by Theodore Roosevelt in 1901. But Eleanor made the White House even more inclusive. As early as 1934, she was making her social agenda clear by inviting both political friends like Mary McLeod Bethune and Walter White and everyday African Americans to the private quarters of the White House for meals and other social events.

This continued throughout the president's time in office. The "People's House," as the building has been nicknamed, became socially integrated. One of her guests was her correspondent and now a social activist and Howard University law student, Pauli Murray. The young woman and the First Lady often challenged each other's opinions. Though they agreed on big issues, there was a generational rift, with Eleanor sometimes urging moderation and caution on the impatient Pauli, whom the First Lady once dubbed "a firebrand."

The day Pauli was invited for the first time to the White House for tea in 1943 was full of mishaps. The aunt who was to accompany her had taken ill, so she invited a friend. The friend's husband showed up on an army leave unexpectedly, so Pauli made arrangements with the White House for him to attend. But then he decided his uniform was too wrinkled for such an important occasion, so teatime had to be pushed back once more. When the trio arrived at the White House, they realized they had forgotten their admission cards!

Pauli was exhausted and embarrassed by the time the First Lady greeted them and led her guests outside to a table on the South Portico. There, she later remembered, the comforting smell of magnolia trees and honeysuckle calmed her down. Eleanor's sensible ease made Pauli think she might appreciate the story of why they were so late. Sure enough, the First Lady, listening to Pauli rattle off the disasters, "burst into spontaneous laughter."

Pauli would go on to do important things as a lawyer, writer, activist, cofounder of the National Organization for Women, and the first African American Episcopal priest. Her friendship with Eleanor endured.

During the first eight years of her husband's administration, the First Lady spent many hours visiting black schools and churches and speaking at conventions of black organizations. Though she had support from the public in many quarters—for instance, 64 percent of those polled approved of her resignation from the DAR—a wide swath of people across the country vilified her, and in the nastiest of terms, because of her stand on civil rights. Eleanor's response was often to invoke the Golden Rule to try to make these critics understand that they should treat others, no matter their race, as they would like to be treated.

One of the events that caused a stir was a party she threw for black girls from a local reform school. When she had toured the school, she found the conditions there deplorable. She invited some of the girls to a lawn party at the White House, where cake and lemonade was served. Eleanor received much criticism over the invitation, but she mildly replied, "I feel if these girls are ever to be rehabilitated and, as far as possible, returned into community living prepared to meet the difficulties of life, they need much more than they are getting. Therefore, it seems to me as every young person enjoys an occasional good time, these youngsters should have an occasional good time."

In 1938, she received a letter from a woman who was upset after seeing a photograph of the First Lady serving food to a black child at a Hyde Park picnic. Eleanor wrote back in her commonsense way: "Surely you would not have refused to let her eat with the other [visitors] . . . I believe it never hurts to be kind."

Her involvement with the cause of African Americans'

civil rights did not mean she had forgotten about other people who needed her help. During Franklin's second term, the First Lady kept her eye on the plight of immigrants, issues affecting the poor, especially as they concerned the New Deal, affordable housing, and she did everything she could to fight the discouragement of the young. This kept her popularity high among the majority of the public.

The Depression continued throughout the 1930s. Sometimes the economy was better, then it would sputter again—1937 was a particularly bad year when unemployment rose sharply. Still, most people, thanks to the aid of the federal government and its New Deal programs, felt more optimistic.

That didn't mean African Americans were getting their fair share of New Deal programs and jobs; often they were not, despite Eleanor's efforts. Still, some white people across the country felt she was doing too much for African Americans.

The First Lady was particularly disliked in the South, where her liberal stands on race offended the very fabric of that society. Lies were spread about her—it was whispered she was starting "Eleanor Clubs" that encouraged black women to quit their jobs as maids—but her own actions were quite enough to raise ire. Sometimes, it was the mildest of events that made people mad. Even a photograph of Eleanor giving a little African American girl a flower from a bouquet the child had presented to the First Lady was used against her throughout the South. Ironically, the same picture was also distributed in the North in African American communities to show them her solidarity.

ELEANOR'S FRIENDS AND FOES AGREED ABOUT ONE THING: SHE WAS TIRELESS. SHE ALWAYS SEEMED TO HAVE TIME FOR ONE MORE APPEARANCE OR TO ANSWER ONE MORE LETTER. HER VISIT TO THE NATIONAL YOUTH ADMINISTRATION IN MAINE IN JULY 1941 SHOWED HER CONTINUED COMMITMENT TO NEW DEAL PROGRAMS.

No matter the criticism she received, the First Lady was determined to keep traveling throughout the country pushing back on the injustices she saw. "Eleanor Everywhere"—that was her nickname. Everywhere even included prison. In her autobiography, she told the story of the time she had to leave the White House for a Baltimore prison visit so early that she didn't have time to say good morning to her husband. Franklin asked her assistant where she was, and the woman replied, "Prison." The president smilingly shook his head. "I'm not surprised, but what for?"

There was an unfortunate personal aspect to the criticism Eleanor received. Often those who railed against her interests and goals, both press columnists and private citizens, also made fun of her looks, her voice, and her mannerisms. Newspaper cartoons emphasized her buck teeth and weak chin.

But Eleanor was smart enough not to show her detractors she cared. She would laugh off unflattering photos and paved the way for other women who wanted to be in the public eye by telling them not to take anything personally and to "develop skin as tough as a rhinoceros hide."

9

WAR CLOUDS

During President Roosevelt's second term, a huge dark cloud was looming on the horizon: war. Across the Pacific, Japan was arming itself and preparing to invade China. Across the Atlantic, Adolf Hitler and his Nazi Party had risen to power in Germany. The Nazis were terrorizing their country's Jewish population and casting covetous eyes on neighboring countries. Germany annexed the Rhineland in 1936 and then Austria in 1938. It took Czechoslovakia in 1939. When Germany invaded Poland in 1939, England and France, who had a mutual protection pact with Poland, declared war on Germany.

HITLER AND OFFICERS STAND IN FRONT OF THE EIFFEL TOWER
AFTER THE NAZIS STORMED INTO PARIS IN JUNE 1940.

President Roosevelt understood that he would have to pre-pare the United States for war, even though there was strong sentiment against fighting a war in Europe. There had been more than fifty thousand U.S. combat deaths in World War I (and a total of more than ten million military deaths for all countries), and the feeling in the United States was one of iso-lationism. Americans did not want to fight foreign wars.

Franklin had to be careful how he presented the issue

of foreign affairs to the public. It was like walking a political tightrope. He had to strengthen the country and ready it for war if war should come. But he was also considering something no other president had ever done—running for a third term in office. He had to convince the potential voters of the 1940 election that war was neither inevitable nor his first choice as a course of action.

As the world situation grew increasingly tense, the First Lady was also worried. She had seen firsthand the horrors caused by World War I. But she was also well aware of the tragedies that were unfolding in Europe and elsewhere. On a personal level, she was concerned because she had four sons who would be eligible for military service. Her children were all grown by now. Their childhoods, which they remembered as troubled, had not made them happy adults. All five experienced marriage, divorce, and remarriage. They sometimes felt torn between their parents, especially Anna, who was a confidant to both Eleanor and Franklin. The Roosevelts had five grandchildren by 1939, with more to come. Eleanor worked hard to be a more confident and compassionate grandmother than she had been a mother.

She decided the best thing she could do at this time was

to be more "everywhere" than ever, hitting the road on speaking tours where she discussed everything from foster care to New Deal progress to civil liberties. As with her former racial bigotry, it had not been unknown for Eleanor to display the strains of anti-Semitism she had grown up with and that were prevalent throughout the United States. Now, however, after all that she had seen and heard, her eyes were wide open to the horror of prejudice.

In a major speech delivered to the American Civil Liberties Union in March 1940, she said that religious and racial prejudice "are a great menace because we find that in countries where civil liberties have been lost, religious and race prejudice are rampant." Freedoms of speech, of religion, of the press, and the freedom to follow one's own conscience were precious and needed to be defended not just by the government, but by everyone. These truths, as she saw them, became Eleanor's moral pillars for the rest of her life.

With the turbulent world situation, Eleanor understood why the president had to focus his attention on foreign affairs. But she was also concerned that domestic problems like civil rights would fade into the background as events heated up in Europe and around the world.

She was right. World events did inevitably take center stage. But there were also many civil rights issues that affected the run up to World War II, and Eleanor was ready to offer her help as always. As one historian put it, "Eleanor refused to be insulated and shielded from a problem. The more perilous it was politically, the more twisted its roots in history, custom, and law, the more urgent [she thought] that it be ferreted out, confronted, and dealt with."

Racial injustice was one of those problems that not only affected people at home, but also elicited an uncomfortable and unwelcome response in the world. Adolf Hitler, for instance, pointed out that the United States had little standing to complain about Germany's treatment of Jews when it had such a sorry record on its black citizens. Eleanor sorrowfully noted his point: "It seems incredible when we are protesting the happenings in Germany to permit intolerance such as this in our own country."

Despite the prejudice African Americans faced in the United States, they answered the call to serve their country in times of war. African Americans had fought in all American wars. Through the Civil War, they fought in both all-black and integrated units. After the Civil War, segregation entered the armed services. Nevertheless, thousands of African Americans volunteered to fight during World War I. Few, however, saw combat because the army believed they were more suited to manual labor than fighting. After the war, interest in serving plummeted, and the number of African Americans in the armed services was dismal.

The situation in the navy was uniquely unfair. Young black men were in the service, but they were only allowed to be messmen. As messmen, all they were allowed to do was make beds, do laundry, and perform menial tasks for other sailors. In essence, they were servants—with no chance for advancement.

In September 1940, Congress passed the Selective Training and Service Act. It required men between the ages of twenty-one and thirty-five to register with their local draft boards. The armed services were also encouraging men to enlist. Nevertheless, not everyone was being encouraged.

Eleanor began to receive letters and hear about the indignities—and sometimes the dangers—that faced African American men who wanted the right to fight. A letter came from a doctor who was refused a commission because he was black. A high school teacher, in Charlotte, North Carolina, who had gone to a recruitment center to get information for his students, was beaten by whites. A dentist who came to enlist was informed, "Hell, if you said you were colored I would have saved you a trip . . . There are no colored dentists in the Dental Corps."

One group of enlisted men decided to make their dissatisfaction known. Fifteen navy messmen wrote an open letter to the *Pittsburgh Courier*, a black newspaper. "Our main reason for writing is to let all our colored mothers and fathers know how their sons are treated after taking an oath pledging allegiance and loyalty to their flag and country. . . ." The letter went on to describe what awaited African Americans in the navy and advised parents not to let their sons join. They ended by saying, "We take it upon ourselves to write this letter regardless of any action the Navy authorities may take."

The authorities were quick to take action. The men were jailed and then dishonorably discharged from the navy. That didn't stop messmen from other ships from writing their own letters in solidarity detailing their own similar experiences.

Congress did pass a law in 1940 that made it easier for African Americans to enlist in the armed services, but there were provisions in the law that also made it likely they could also be turned down. For instance, the law said men inducted into the army had to be deemed "acceptable," a nebulous term that could be used to turn black enlistees away. Civil rights leaders wanted to make sure there would be some teeth in this law.

Eleanor urged a White House meeting. Nothing happened. So in September of 1940, she wrote a pointed memo to her husband from the Greenwich Village apartment she kept in New York. She'd just finished speaking to a conference of African Americans. She'd begun her speech, "You know, better than any other people, that [American Democracy] is not perfect . . ." But she told the audience how hopeful she felt that Americans were moving along "the road to better understanding." Finally, she pledged her "faith and cooperation to make this a better country."

In writing to Franklin, she told him that public sentiment was growing among blacks and whites about the unfairness that was apparent in the armed services. Eleanor also noted, "This is going to be very bad politically, besides being intrinsically wrong."

The president listened. He called a meeting for September 27, 1940. Among the participants was A. Philip Randolph, "a commanding figure," who had organized the Brotherhood of Sleeping Car Porters (the first labor union led by African

Americans) in the face of great obstacles. Walter White was also there. Walter, interestingly, had been pushing a proposal to have a volunteer, integrated army, since there were many white men who said they *were* willing to serve alongside blacks. Also attending were the secretary of the navy, Frank Knox, and assistant secretary of war, Robert Patterson.

ELEANOR WITH A. PHILIP RANDOLPH (LEFT) AND NEW YORK MAYOR FIORELLO LA GUARDIA

Randolph told the assembled group that blacks felt they weren't wanted in the services. White "emphasized that . . . an army . . . fighting allegedly for democracy should be the last place to find undemocratic segregation."

Franklin tried to counter by saying the new law passed by Congress would give blacks more opportunities to serve, but Randolph pointed out the law's deficiencies. The president offered a few suggestions that seemed to indicate he was moving forward on the issue of integrating the services, and Randolph and White left with high hopes for progress. Nevertheless, the military men in attendance, and others who had gotten wind of the meeting, all gave a thumbs-down to the idea of integration.

One of the army's top generals, George Marshall, deplored the idea of "experiments which would have a highly destructive effect on morale." Secretary of the Navy Knox firmly told the president that his job was to prepare the navy for a war on two oceans. If he had to spend his time trying to integrate it as well, he would have to resign.

DESPITE THE CONTROVERSY OVER INTEGRATING THE ARMED SERVICES, AFRICAN AMERICANS WERE INSTRUMENTAL IN THE FIGHT TO WIN WORLD WAR II. HERE, MILES DAVIS KING, A CREWMAN ON THE *U.S.S. TULAGI* CARRIES A LOADED MAGAZINE FOR HIS GUN EN ROUTE TO SOUTHERN FRANCE IN 1944.

A week after the meeting was held, nobody was satisfied. Randolph and White had heard nothing from the White House. Once again they asked the First Lady to intervene, which she did, but the statement the War Department finally issued merely said that Negro units would be formed in the major branches of the services and that there would eventually be a flight training program for blacks.

And then this blow: "The policy of the War Department is not to intermingle colored and white enlisted personnel . . . This policy has been proved satisfactory over a long period of years . . . to make changes would produce situations destructive to morale." Integration of the armed forces, the policy said, was not in the best interest of the country or of national defense.

This caused an uproar in the African American community. Adding insult to injury, one of the president's advisers made it seem as if the civil rights leaders at the meeting were in agreement with the War Department's statement—which they certainly were not!

Franklin had to issue a statement denying this was the case, but that was just a small bandage on a big problem. The NAACP encouraged its members to organize protests. The

1940 election was just around the corner, and the president again needed black votes. He quickly promoted one of the only blacks of high rank in the army, Colonel Benjamin Davis, to brigadier general and gave assurances that desegregation options were still being looked at.

These efforts calmed things somewhat in the African American community, but sentiment was also running high in other parts of the country that did not want integration. The president and First Lady once again received angry letters, some calling them horrible names. Nevertheless, Franklin Delano Roosevelt did win his third presidential term in 1940. The race against Republican Wendell Willkie, who was for integration of the armed services, was hotly contested, but Franklin won handily. Still, after the election, some of Eleanor's closest friends in the African American community remained angry about the president's hesitations on civil rights issues.

Pauli Murray wrote to the president and First Lady comparing Franklin, who used "vague and general language" about race, to Willkie, who clearly stated racial prejudice was like "imperialism."

Eleanor fought back. "I wonder if it ever occurred to you

that Mr. Willkie has no responsibility whatsoever? He can say whatever he likes and do whatever he likes, and nothing very serious will happen." Had he been elected president, she noted sharply, Willkie would have had to deal with the Southern bloc in Congress and angry segments of the public, just as Franklin did. She let her personal bitterness show when she added that for someone as well versed in the political system as Pauli, "your letter seems to me one of the most thoughtless I've ever read."

In her reply, Pauli admitted that, yes, her letter was rude and reckless. But it was written from a place of "desperation and disgust." She wrote a long letter, detailing her frustrations, and the First Lady's anger softened. She invited Pauli to New York to talk things over in person. A nervous Pauli was relieved when Eleanor greeted her at the door of her apartment with a hug. She had come to argue but left with her "militant armor replaced by unreserved affection." They agreed to continue their dialogue.

President Roosevelt spent a good deal of time during the first two years of his unprecedented third term trying to rally support for England, which was virtually alone in the fight after Belgium, Luxembourg, and the Netherlands were invaded by Germany in May of 1940. France was lost in June. Germany turned on its ally, the Soviet Union, invading in June of 1941. It seemed inevitable that the United States would soon be dragged into another world war.

Just as the armed services needed to be mobilized, the defense industries that would build the ships and planes, manufacture guns and ammunition, and provide numerous other necessities of war, had to be beefed up. This meant that for the first time since 1929, there would now be plenty of jobs, and African Americans expected they would benefit. Individual lives and whole communities would be vastly improved with more employment opportunities. Many African Americans had been trained in New Deal programs for more skilled jobs, and were now ready to take them.

But instead of opportunity, what they often received was more racism. One Kansas City steel company noted that they hadn't had a black employee in twenty-five years and didn't intend to start now. An aviation company stated that "Negroes will be considered only as janitors."

There were many ways of keeping people out of jobs. Black applicants would receive high scores on defense companies' entrance exams, but they still wouldn't be hired, or they'd be pushed aside by whites who had much lower scores or who had no training at all. This happened throughout the country.

The African American community decided to take things into their own hands. A. Philip Randolph went to several civil rights groups, including the NAACP and the Urban League, with an idea. They would organize a ten-thousand-man march on Washington, right down Pennsylvania Avenue between the White House and the Capitol building, to protest racial discrimination in war industries, as well as the larger issue of segregation.

There were doubters among some who Randolph approached. Could ten thousand people really be counted on? But in African American communities, the enthusiasm for the march grew. This was a chance for people who felt they were being ignored to make their voices heard. Randolph upped the number of how many would come to Washington, D.C., on July 1, 1941, to march. Now it would be one hundred thousand!

This caught the White House's attention. The last thing Franklin wanted was a massive march in a summer-hot city that could lead to violence. Eleanor, who had been speaking at African American colleges and other venues during the spring, apprised the president of what was happening in the black community. Eleanor told Franklin about how upset people were about the difficulties they had getting access to defense jobs, and he agreed that the walls put up against them weren't fair.

As July 1 grew closer, it became clear to those in the Roosevelt administration that the march was happening. The president had already taken the unheard-of step of making, as one historian put it, "the first official call for what later became known as affirmative action." He wrote his aides ordering them to take "Negroes up to a certain percentage in factory order work. Judge them on quality." The president didn't like the fact that "first-class Negroes are turned down for third-class white boys."

This request went out to companies, but Randolph and others knew the time for requests was over. Eleanor was not in favor of the march. She too worried that there would be violence on the streets of Washington. The First Lady made direct pleas, in meetings and in person, to call off the march. Randolph, while appreciating her position, declined. Finally Franklin agreed once again to schedule a meeting between Randolph, Walter White, and members of his administration.

It took place at the White House on June 18, a few weeks before the march. As usual, Franklin tried to charm and placate Randolph and White, but Randolph remained firm. When asked by the president what he wanted done, Randolph replied, "We want you to issue an executive order making it mandatory that Negros be permitted to work in these plants."

The president demurred. He couldn't do it. What if other groups asked for the same thing?

Well, one of his aides who was present wondered, so what if they did? Maybe it would be best to include *all* groups in the executive order.

The negotiating went back and forth over the next day. Eleanor became involved, too. She was up on remote Campobello Island, but she walked the half mile down to the telegraph office where there was a telephone to read the last draft to Randolph. Executive Order 8802 stated that both employers and labor unions were "to provide for the full and equitable participation of all workers in defense industries, without discrimination because of race, creed, color, or national origin." A Fair Employment Practice Committee would be set up to oversee the order.

The one-hundred-thousand-man march was called off.

10

FIGHTING AND DYING

Adate which will live in infamy." That's how Franklin described December 7, 1941, the day Japan launched a devastating air attack on U.S. naval ships and military facilities at Pearl Harbor, Hawaii. He spoke these words the following day as he asked a joint session of Congress for a declaration of war. Within an hour of his speech, Congress issued that declaration. Four days later, Germany and Italy declared war on the United States.

For Americans, World War II had officially begun.

Isolationism was now forgotten, and men all over the country went to their local recruitment offices to enlist. In the first years of the war, black men—volunteers and those who were drafted—were usually assigned to service units that helped supply and maintain troops on the front lines. As the war dragged on, the government needed men, black and white, to take the place of fallen infantrymen, pilots, and officers. Still, throughout the war, the problem of segregation remained.

From the first moments of battle, servicemen of color distinguished themselves. The argument that black men in the navy were only capable of being messmen was turned on its head when one of the heroes of Pearl Harbor was a black sailor, Dorie Miller. Miller carried his captain through raging flames to safety, and then without weapons training, picked up a machine gun and began firing at Japanese planes. At first, the navy only wanted to give him a commendation for his actions, but on May 11, 1942, Franklin approved the Navy Cross for Miller, that service's third-highest award at the time.

World War II brought almost unbelievable stresses for Franklin and Eleanor. On a personal level, there was concern about their four sons serving in the armed forces. Elliott in the Army Air Corps, James in the Marine Corps, and Franklin Jr. and John in the navy. Eleanor said, "I imagine every mother felt as I did when I said goodbye to the children during the war. I had a feeling that I might be saying goodbye for the last time."

In the fall of 1941, Sara died at age eighty-seven. Franklin keenly felt the loss of the mother who adored him. Eleanor was sympathetic, but her feelings about Sara remained unresolved. "I kept being appalled at myself because I couldn't feel any real grief," Eleanor told her daughter, Anna, and that seemed "terrible" after their long relationship.

Just a few weeks later, Eleanor had the emotional task of sitting by the bedside of her dying brother, Hall, who had battled alcoholism for decades. "My idea of hell, if I believed in it, would be to . . . watch someone breathing hard, struggling for words . . . and thinking this was once the little boy I played with and scolded. He could have been so much and this is what he is . . . in spite of everything, I've loved Hall . . ."

Meanwhile, the fate of the world was on Franklin's shoulders. There was no guarantee that the United States and its allies, Great Britain and the Soviet Union, would win the war.

Instead of the war drawing the president and the First Lady closer together, it pulled them apart. Franklin was, naturally, consumed with war plans. Eleanor didn't know how to make herself useful in this new situation. Sometimes, she vehemently opposed his decisions.

In February 1942, Franklin signed an executive order that

effectively allowed the internment of Americans of Japanese descent. Even though they had done nothing wrong, because they looked the same as America's enemies, they were considered a danger. More than one hundred thousand Japanese Americans would eventually be moved from their homes, lose their property, and be relocated in camps.

JAPANESE AMERICANS WAITING TO BE TAKEN TO AN INTERNMENT CAMP IN SALINAS, CALIFORNIA

Eleanor disagreed with internment, wrote against it, and visited a Japanese camp to observe the conditions in 1943. She made a short speech there that noted while she could understand "the bitterness" of those who had lost loved ones to the

Japanese enemy, she felt that the issues of Japanese Americans must be looked at "objectively . . . for the honor of our country." For the First Lady, that meant emptying the camps as soon as possible. Though some camp residents began to leave at the end of that year, the camps were not fully closed until 1946.

There was also disagreement with the president on the subject of refugees. She had been interested since the late 1930s in helping Jewish refugees trying to escape Hitler's Germany find a home in the United States. But until the bombing of Pearl Harbor, public opinion remained isolationist and unwelcoming of refugees. The United States took in about one hundred thousand refugees from 1933 to 1940. This was a larger number than any other country, but only a small percentage of those trying to flee.

Eleanor focused her efforts on bringing Jewish children to the United States from Europe. Franklin didn't spend much time on the problem of European Jews specifically, maintaining the best way to save the Jews was to win the war. Nevertheless, by 1943 both Roosevelts knew what much of the public did not: The Jews were not just being taken to labor camps as Nazi propaganda claimed. They were being systematically murdered.

Eleanor was greatly disturbed by Franklin's tightening of

immigration laws, which his administration said reduced the chance of Nazi spies entering the country. Of course, it also reduced the number of frantic refugees. In 1941, Eleanor said to a friend, "One of the things that troubles me is that when people are in trouble, whether it's the dust bowl or the miners . . . the first people who come forward and try to help are the Jews. Now in these terrible days . . . why they don't they come [to help the Jewish people]?"

ELEANOR SAW FOR HERSELF THE DESTRUCTION THAT NAZI BOMBS HAD CAUSED LONDON WHEN SHE VISITED IN 1942.

Feeling her presence at home was not helpful to her husband, Eleanor spent time traveling during the war years. She made a three-week goodwill trip to England in 1942, winning friends among the British people.

DURING A TRIP TO ENGLAND IN 1942, ELEANOR MET WITH KING GEORGE VI AND QUEEN ELIZABETH.

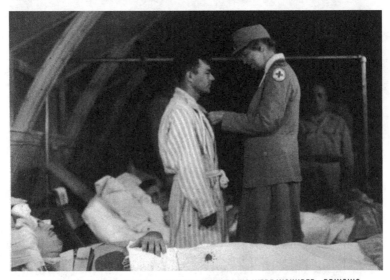

ELEANOR VISITED THE TROOPS—ESPECIALLY THOSE WHO WERE WOUNDED—BRINGING
THEM COMFORT AND THE SINCERE THANKS OF THE PRESIDENT FOR THEIR SACRIFICES.

In 1943 she took a controversial trip to the Pacific theater of war, where the fighting was especially intense. The admirals and generals thought her trip would be a nuisance, but her visits with the service people in the field and those injured in hospitals brought comfort and a bit of home to them—and

ELEANOR FLEW MORE THAN 23,000 MILES IN THE ARMY TRANSPORT PLANE TO PLACES THROUGHOUT THE SOUTH PACIFIC, FROM NEW ZEALAND TO FIJI TO AUSTRALIA.

admiration for her. One soldier who heard her speak said, "We liked this speech . . . it was good to hear a kind lady saying nice things." Even Admiral William Halsey, one of her most vocal critics, later admitted, "She did more good than any other person or group of civilians, who passed through my area."

Yet even with her nonstop travels, the "Negro" question, as it was called then, was never long out of Eleanor's mind. In the United States, there was continued racial unrest during the war years. There were still lynchings, prejudice in hiring and employment, and segregation throughout American society. Eleanor continued to work alongside African American leaders in their fight for civil rights.

One issue that caught her attention occurred in Detroit, Michigan. The Sojourner Truth housing project was built for blacks working in defense industries, but white workers demanded the housing for themselves. At the request of civil rights leaders, Eleanor lobbied her husband, and eventually—after violent racial encounters—the project was given to its intended residents. Later in 1943, more racial rioting broke out in Detroit, and some put the blame directly on the First Lady, accusing her of trying too hard to mix the races and the "coddling of Negroes." Used to attacks, Eleanor replied, "I suppose when one is being forced to realize that an unwelcome change is coming, one must blame it on someone or something."

Letters continued to flood the White House accusing the First Lady of being a troublemaker who stirred the pot of racial division. Most of the criticism came from whites, but African Americans also didn't like the way she sometimes counseled restraint or patience. One historian later said she could, at times, "sound patronizing." The president, as usual, was content to let Eleanor take much of the heat on the issue of civil rights so he could continue running the war and the country.

One of the knottiest racial problems concerned the armed services in the South, where transportation and use of base facilities was a big issue for black military personnel. These service people now included African American women. In 1942, Congress approved the creation of the Women's Army Auxiliary Corps. These women served as stenographers, postal clerks, and truck drivers, as well as in other noncombat roles. African American women served in segregated units. Two of the training centers for the WAACs were in the South, one in Georgia, another in Louisiana.

Since buses and trains in the South were segregated, black service people were often at the back of the line when it came to getting tickets. If they didn't return to their bases on time, they were considered AWOL—away without official leave—and penalized.

In other cases, blacks were at stations where they couldn't buy food because there were no segregated facilities and they weren't allowed to eat with whites. In one instance, German prisoners of war were served in a station lunchroom because they were white, while black Americans had to eat in the kitchen! It's no wonder the soldiers asked themselves what kind of democracy they were fighting for. All this was particularly shocking for African Americans who had been raised in the North and hadn't had to live under stringent Jim Crow laws.

Eleanor fought hard to make sure the War Department looked at the busing situation. She noted, "These colored boys lie side by side in the hospitals . . . with the white boys and somehow it is hard for me to believe that they should not be treated on an equal basis."

At last, the War Department agreed with her. On July 8, 1944, they issued a directive stating all transportation owned and operated by the government would be available to all military personnel regardless of race and regardless of local customs. This did not cover private transportation companies, but it was a big first step.

In 1944, further progress was made in desegregating the navy. A new secretary of the navy, James Forrestal, had ambitious plans for integration. Although by now the navy had allowed blacks to serve as more than messmen, these new jobs did not, as a rule, place them on ships. Instead, black sailors were often placed at docks, moving equipment and loading ships.

A tragedy occurred in Port Chicago, California, in July of 1944, as six hundred men, mostly black, were loading ammunition and bombs onto ships. A giant explosion destroyed the pier and killed more than two hundred black sailors and injured hundreds more. This event spurred Secretary of the Navy Forrestal to move even more quickly on with his plans. His directive on "Negro Naval Personnel" stated that no inherent differences existed between blacks and whites and that each member of the navy would be trained according to his abilities and promoted on the basis of his performance.

Eleanor was pleased with the forward motion, but there was one branch of the service that had her personal attention: the first unit of black combat pilots, the Ninety-

Ninth Pursuit Squadron. Trained in Tuskegee, Alabama, near the Tuskegee Institute founded by Booker T. Washington, they were also known as the Tuskegee Airmen.

The program had been initiated in 1941 after a black pilot who had been denied a place in the Army Air Corps won a legal battle, and a combat-training program for blacks was court ordered. Though obligated to train black pilots, there was nothing that said the Army Air Corps had to use them. So by 1942, not one of the thousand pilots that had been trained had seen active service.

The First Lady was well aware of this situation—demoralizing to the men involved, and wasteful when it came to helping the war effort. She wrote several times to the secretary of war, but still the airmen sat idle. Eleanor wanted to show her concern personally and struck up correspondences with both faculty and random airmen. She was particularly taken with one of the young fliers, Cecil Peterson, and asked him to keep her informed about how things were going. They wrote back and forth for three years. Cecil told her, "Your letters and gifts are inspiring and have prompted me to be a better soldier." He also asked her to tell the president, "there's a private down here rooting for him."

As a more public display of support, Eleanor went flying with Charles A. Anderson, a Tuskegee Airman, in Alabama and insisted a photograph be taken. The news got national coverage, and the First Lady used the picture and reporting to convince the president to activate the Tuskegee Airmen's unit.

Finally, in 1943, the Tuskegee Airmen were sent overseas to fight in both North Africa and Europe. They performed brilliantly. In over fifteen hundred missions, they shot down more than two hundred enemy aircraft without losing any of their own planes to enemy fire. As a group, the Tuskegee Airmen won over one hundred Distinguished Flying Cross medals.

A turning point in World War II came on June 6, 1944. The Allied forces, one hundred fifty thousand strong, landed on the beaches of Normandy, France, and went on to liberate Europe.

If running for a third term was unprecedented, running for a fourth presidential term was almost unthinkable. Franklin, however, was determined to see the war to a successful conclusion as president. On November 7, with Harry S. Truman as his running mate, he won once more.

But Franklin was ailing. Polio—and its long-term effects on his body—was just one of his medical issues. He suffered

from high blood pressure, coronary heart disease, and conges-
tive heart failure, all exacerbated by his chain-smoking and
his stress. Just a few months after his inauguration, he died at
his retreat in Warm Springs, Georgia, on April 12, 1945. He did
not live to see the Allies' victory over Germany only a month
later in May 1945. In August, victory over Japan was achieved
after the dropping of atomic bombs on the Japanese cities of
Hiroshima and Nagasaki.

Though Franklin had been suffering with many ailments,
all of which contributed to his worsening health, he died from
a cerebral hemorrhage while having his portrait painted. Eleanor was at a speaking engagement when she was told to return
to the White House immediately. "I did not even ask why," she
later remembered. "In my heart I knew . . ." Anna and her husband, John Boettiger, along with presidential aide Steve Early
gave her the news. As for the four Roosevelt sons, they were all
on active duty in war zones. She cabled them with the news.
"He did his job to the end as he would want you to do. Bless
you all, and all our love."

Eleanor, along with Steve Early and the president's personal physician, flew to Warm Springs to escort the body home
by train. As Franklin's coffin left Warm Springs, the president's

friend Graham Jackson, an African American musician, took out his accordion and played the mournful spiritual "Goin' Home."

As the train rolled along the tracks back to Washington, Eleanor looked out the window and was gratified to see people, black and white, waving and holding signs of sympathy. The comfort of those signs was marred by the news offered by one gossipy Roosevelt cousin who had been present when the president died. Franklin had not been alone, she informed Eleanor. At his side was his old love, Lucy Mercer Rutherfurd.

This information blindsided Eleanor. Franklin's long-ago promise to her, that he would never again see Lucy, had been broken. Now she was learning this news at a moment of intense grief. She was further upset to find out her daughter, Anna, had facilitated a number of visits between him and Lucy at the White House over the years at her father's request.

Eleanor didn't have too much time to dwell on this betrayal, though she did confront Anna when she returned with the president's body to the White House. Her daughter tried to make her understand that she had been caught between two parents, but Anna worried her strong bond with Eleanor was now severely strained.

The next days were hectic. Eleanor had to plan the funeral and move out of the White House so the new president and his family could move in. When now-president Truman asked Eleanor if there was anything he could do for her, she replied, "Is there anything we can do for you? For you are the one in trouble now."

Franklin's funeral, with two hundred friends and relatives in attendance, took place in the East Room of the White House. His body, accompanied by Eleanor, was then taken by train to be buried in the garden of his beloved Hyde Park estate. Along the route, just as on the journey from Georgia to Washington, Americans of all colors, religions, and creeds stood alongside the tracks, crying and holding American flags. At his burial, Eleanor asked that the last words he had written in a speech that he never gave be included: "The only limit to our realization of tomorrow will be our doubts of today. Let us move forward with strong and active faith."

On April 20, 1945, Eleanor left the White House. Now a widow, no longer the First Lady, when she arrived at her apartment in New York City, she was startled to see a group of reporters at her door.

Eleanor shooed them away. "The story is over."

11

TURNING THE PAGE

But the story was not over. A sixty-year-old woman as engaged and vital as Eleanor Roosevelt was not going to stay at home with her beloved knitting. A new chapter of her life was just beginning.

In December of 1945, President Truman asked Eleanor to be one of the United States delegates to the newly formed United Nations, which was about to hold its first meeting in London. At first, Eleanor said no. Then, after prodding from the president, she said she would think about it. Finally, "with fear and trembling," she said yes. She realized that, as someone who hated war and loved peace and who felt strongly that the countries of the world should function as neighbors not adversaries, she had much to bring to the table.

Her male counterparts on the delegation—and they were all males—saw it differently. Some of them disagreed with her politically, and some of them didn't like her personally. Eleanor was fully aware that sexism was also part of the equation. She knew "that as the only woman, I had better be better than anybody else . . . I knew that if I in any way failed, that it would not just be my failure. It would be the failure of all women. . . ."

The hostility against Eleanor was evident from the first. The men on the committee made snide comments, and in meetings, they often ignored her opinion. But Eleanor wasn't one to be ignored. She continued to speak up and make her points.

As one of her UN assignments, she was the U.S. representative tasked with tackling the massive worldwide refugee problem. Close to a million people had been displaced during the war. The Soviet Union demanded that Soviet refugees and refugees from countries that were now in their sphere of influence, like Poland and Hungary, be returned to their home countries. But many of those refugees did not want to live under those repressive Soviet regimes. Others, who had

ELEANOR ADDRESSING THE GENERAL ASSEMBLY AT THE UNITED NATIONS IN JULY 1947

spoken against the Soviet Union or communism, feared they would be imprisoned or killed.

Eleanor's Soviet counterpart on the committee insisted these refugees be returned, but thanks to her ability to debate and persuade, the United Nations General Assembly voted to allow refugees to live where they preferred. This was a big victory for refugees' freedom of movement and for Eleanor herself. Her biggest critic in her delegation, U.S. senator Arthur Vandenberg, was finally persuaded as well. He now saw Eleanor's talent and value. "I want to take back everything I ever said about her," he declared, "and believe me it's been plenty!"

The UN delegation, on which she served for six years, wasn't Eleanor's only area of activity. As always, her concerns were wide and varied. She took great interest in the Jewish victims of the Holocaust and lobbied for the Jewish people to have their own state. Israel was recognized by the United States in 1948.

ALTHOUGH A SUPPORTER OF ISRAEL, ELEANOR ALSO SPOKE OF AND WROTE ABOUT HER CONCERNS FOR THE COUNTRY'S ARAB POPULATION. HERE SHE VISITS WITH A BEDOUIN BOY IN BEERSHEBA, ISRAEL, IN 1959.

She also traveled the world to see the living conditions of women and offer her support for women's rights. She visited with heads of states. At home she joined a board that oversaw Wiltwyck, a school for abused boys. After so many years in the public eye, she knew how to gather support for the causes she believed in, through her writings, her speeches, and media appearances.

ONE OF THE POSTS ELEANOR TOOK ON AFTER FRANKLIN'S DEATH WAS BOARD MEMBER OF THE WILTWYCK SCHOOL FOR BOYS. IN 1947, SHE BROUGHT A GROUP OF BOYS TO VAL-KILL FOR A PICNIC.

But despite her many concerns and interests, she never neglected the fight for civil rights. After their contributions to winning World War II, African Americans were unwilling to go backward. The issue heated up during the 1950s and '60s. African Americans were sick and tired of segregation. They wanted full voting rights, educational and employment equality, and the same access to public facilities that was available to whites. Black citizens were entitled to the Declaration of Independence's promise of "life, liberty, and the pursuit of happiness." It was time—past time.

Eleanor Roosevelt remained active in the cause she had taken up while she was First Lady. And with Franklin gone, she no longer had to worry about political concerns. She joined the boards of the NAACP and CORE (the Congress of Racial Equality) to help the progress of the civil rights movement. She used her influence with Harry Truman in 1948 to have him become the first president to speak at the NAACP convention. He made his speech, joined by Eleanor, on the steps of the Lincoln Memorial.

Eleanor continued her "My Day" newspaper column, which she had begun writing in 1935, along with a question-and-answer column in the *Ladies Home Journal* called "If You Ask Me." She used these columns, her other writings, and her speeches to discuss civil rights, trying to explain how discrimination, segregated schools, and efforts to repress the black vote through roadblocks like poll taxes were the opposite of what America should stand for.

During the Montgomery Bus Boycott, when the black citizens of Montgomery, Alabama, refused to ride public transit until it was integrated, she met with Rosa Parks. Parks had sparked the boycott in December 1955 by refusing to move to the back of the bus. Eleanor also worked with Dr. Martin Luther King Jr. to raise money for the boycott.

Dr. King was her first guest on her 1959 television show, *Prospects of Mankind*. And when he was arrested during a protest march and thrown into a Georgia jail in 1960, she defended him in her columns, noting this action would lose the United States respect in the eyes of the world.

IN 1958, ALONG WITH SINGER AND ACTIVIST HARRY BELAFONTE, ELEANOR LOOKS AT ONE OF FRANKLIN'S QUOTES MEMORIALIZED IN BRUSSELS, BELGIUM.

Dr. King admired Eleanor greatly, and she admired him. King's "insistence that there be no hatred in this struggle" was, in her view, "almost more than human beings can achieve." As for his part, he wrote to her in 1962, "Once again, for all you have done, and I'm sure will continue to do to help extend the fruits of Democracy . . . please accept my deep and lasting gratitude."

As the fight for civil rights grew more intense during the early 1960s, Eleanor seesawed between feeling buoyed about the progress that had been made and distressed at the increasing violence against the protesters.

But her own struggle was almost over. In 1960, Eleanor was diagnosed with aplastic anemia, a blood disease. In 1962, she was given a course of steroid drugs that led to her heart failing. She died that year at her home in New York City on November 7, at the age of seventy-eight. The world mourned her death, and Dr. King eulogized her by saying, "The impact of her personality and its unwavering devotion to high principle and purpose cannot be contained in a single day or era."

Three months after her death, her last book, *Tomorrow Is Now*, was published. In it she made her final call to get involved in the civil rights movement: "Staying aloof is not a solution, but a cowardly evasion."

★

Eleanor Roosevelt was no coward. When the FBI informed her in 1958 that the Ku Klux Klan had placed that $25,000 bounty on her head, they told her it would be best if she canceled her appearance at the Highlander Folk School. She thanked them for the information and then made plans to go anyway.

ELEANOR CONDUCTS A CLASS AT THE HIGHLANDER FOLK SCHOOL
AND CHATS WITH THE ATTENDEES.

Eleanor flew to the Nashville airport where she was met by another older woman, and they drove to the Highlander Folk School in rural Tennessee, her pistol on the seat between them. As one historian put it, "And here they are. They are going to go through the Klan. They're going to stand down the Klan . . . they drive up at night through the mountains to this tiny labor school to conduct a workshop on how to break the law."

Fortunately, the Klan didn't confront them. Maybe they knew who they were dealing with.

Until her death, Eleanor Roosevelt probably did more than any other white person to change the course of race relations in the United States. In part, that was because she had access to presidents—not just Franklin, but also Harry Truman and later John F. Kennedy—who had the power to make things happen. But it was also because she was able to explain to everyday citizens, through her speeches, columns, books, radio and television appearances, and even personal letters, how corrosive segregation was, not just to African Americans, but to the country as a whole.

On a more personal note, her friend Pauli Murray said after Eleanor's death, "The great lesson Mrs. R. taught all of us by example was largesse, generosity—her heart seemed to me as big as all the world."

As a child, Eleanor lived in her own world of dreams and terrors. As an adult she fought for what she believed in, overcame her fears and prejudices, and helped others do the same. Perhaps she described her life best: "You gain strength, courage, and confidence by every experience in which you really stop to look fear in the face. You must do the thing which you think you cannot do."

Again and again, Eleanor Roosevelt did just that.

ELEANOR LEAVING LAGUARDIA
AIRPORT IN 1960, SUITCASE IN
HAND, STILL ON THE GO

ELEANOR
IN HER OWN WORDS

EXCERPTS OF "ADDRESS BY MRS. FRANKLIN D. ROOSEVELT—
THE CHICAGO CIVIL LIBERTIES COMMITTEE,"
MARCH 14, 1940*

The numerals in brackets refer to the paragraph number of the speech.

[2] Now we have come here tonight because of civil liberties. I imagine a great many of you could give my talk far better than I because you have first-hand knowledge of the things you have had to do in Chicago, over the years, to preserve civil liberties. But I, perhaps, am more conscious of the importance of civil liberties in this particular moment of our history than anyone else, because, as I travel through the country and meet people and see the things that have happened to little people, I am more and more conscious of what it means to democracy to preserve our civil liberties. All through the years we have had to fight for civil liberty, and we know that there are times when the light grows rather dim. Every time that happens democracy is in danger. Now, largely because of the troubled state of the world as a whole, civil liberties have disappeared in many other countries. It is impossible, of course, to be at war and to maintain freedom of the press, freedom of speech, and freedom of assembly. They disappear automatically. And so, in some countries where ordinarily these rights were inviolate, today they have gone. And in some other countries, even before war came, not only had freedom of the press, freedom of assembly, and freedom of speech disappeared, but also freedom of religion. And so we know that here in this country we have a grave responsibility.

* THE COMPLETE SPEECH MAY BE FOUND AT VOICESOFDEMOCRACY.UMD.EDU/ELEANOR-ROOSEVELT-ADDRESS-BY-MRS-FRANKLIN-D-ROOSEVELT-THE-CHICAGO-CIVIL-LIBERTIES-COMMITTEE-4-MARCH-1950.

[7] There are many times when, even though there is freedom of the press and freedom of speech, it is hard to get a hearing for certain noble causes. I often think that we, all of us, should think very much more carefully than we do about what we mean by freedom of speech, by freedom of the press, by freedom of assembly. I sometimes am much worried by the tendency that exists among certain groups in our country today to consider that these are rights are only for people who think as they do, that they are not rights for the people who disagree with them. I believe that you must apply to all groups the same rights, to all forms of thought, to all forms of expression, the same liberties. Otherwise, you practically deny the fact that you trust the people to choose for themselves, in a majority, what is wise and what is right. And when you do that, you deny the possibility of having a democracy. You have got to be willing to listen, to allow people to state any point of view they may have or to say anything they may believe, and then to trust that, when everyone has had his say, when there has been free discussion and really free, uninfluenced expression in the press, in the end the majority of the people will have the wisdom to decide what is right. We have got to have faith, even when the majority decides wrongly. We must still hold to the fundamental principles that we have laid down and wait for the day to come when the thing that we believe is right becomes the majority way of the people.

[11] I think we should begin much earlier to teach all the children of our nation what a wonderful heritage of freedom they have–of freedom from prejudice–because they live in a nation which is made up of a great variety of other nations. They have before them and around them every day the proof that people can understand each other and can live together amicably, and that races can live on an equal basis even though they may be very different in background, very different in culture. We have an opportunity to teach our children how much we have gained from the coming to this land of all kinds of races, of how much this has served in the

development of the land. Yet somehow I think we have failed in many ways to bring early enough to children how great is their obligation to the various strains that make up the people of the United States. Above all, there should never be race prejudice; there should never be a feeling that one strain is better than another. After all, we are all immigrants–all except Indians, who, we might say, are the only inhabitants of this country who have a real right to say that they own the country. I think that our being composed of so many foreign peoples is the very reason why we should preserve the basic principles of civil liberty. It should be easy for us to live up to our Constitution, but there are many groups among us who do not live up to what was written in that Constitution.

[12] I am very much interested to find that in our younger generation there is a greater consciousness of what civil liberty really means. I think that is one of the hopeful things in the world today: that youth is really taking a tremendous interest in the preservation of civil liberties. It is a very hard period in the world for youth because they are faced with new problems. We don't know the answers to many of the problems that face us today, and neither do the young people. But the problems are very much more important to the young because they must start living. We have had our lives. The young people want to begin, but they can't find a way to get started. Perhaps that has made them more conscious of civil liberties. Perhaps that is why when you get a group of them together, you find them fighting against the prejudices which have grown up in our country, against the prejudices which have made it hard for the minority groups in our country.

[13] The other night someone sent up a question to me: "What do you think should be done about the social standing of the Negro race in this country?" Well, now, of course I think that the social situation is one that has to be dealt with by individuals. The real question that we have to face in this country is: what are we doing about the rights of

a big minority group of citizens in our democracy? That, we all have to face. Any citizen of this country is entitled to equality before the law; to equality of education; to equality at earning a living, as far as his abilities make that possible; to equality of participation in government, so that he may register his opinion in just the way that any other citizen can do. Now, those are basic rights, belonging to every citizen in every minority group. We have got, I think, to stand up and be counted when it comes to the question of whether any minority group is not to have those rights, because the minute we deny any of our basic rights to any citizen, we are preparing the way for the denial of those rights to someone else. Who is going to say it is not right today to do this or that? Who is going to say it is not right tomorrow? And where does it stop? We have to make up our minds as to what we really believe. We have to decide whether we believe in the Bill of Rights, in the Constitution of the United States, or whether we are going to modify it because of the fears that we may have at the moment.

[15] I should like to remind you that behind all those who fight for the Constitution as it was written, for the rights of the weak and for the preservation of civil liberties, there was a long line of courageous people. And that is something to be proud of and something to hold on to. But its only value lies in the premise that we profit by it and continue the tradition in the future; that we do not let those people back of us down; that we have courage; that we do not succumb to fears of any kind; that we live up to the things we believe in; that we see that justice is done to the people under the Constitution, whether they belong to minority groups or not; that we realize that this country is a united country, in which all people have the same rights as citizens; and that we are grateful for that; and finally, that we trust the youth of the nation to herald the real principles of democracy-in-action in this country and to make this even more truly a democratic nation.

TIME LINE

ELEANOR ROOSEVELT'S LIFE
AND MAJOR DOMESTIC AND FOREIGN EVENTS
DURING THAT TIME

1884 Eleanor is born on October 11 in New York City.

1892 Eleanor's mother, Anna, dies, leaving behind three young children.

1893 Eleanor's brother, Elliott Jr., dies.

1894 Eleanor's father, Elliott Sr., commits suicide.

1899 Eleanor embarks on her education at the Allenswood Academy in England.

1901 Vice President Theodore Roosevelt becomes president after President William McKinley is assassinated.

1902 Eleanor returns from Allenswood to make her debut in New York society.

1903 The Wright brothers make their first powered flight at Kitty Hawk, North Carolina.

1905 Eleanor and Franklin Roosevelt are married on March 17, with President Theodore Roosevelt officiating.

1906 Daughter, Anna, is born.

1907 Son James is born.

1908 Henry Ford introduces the Model T automobile.

1909 Son Franklin Jr. is born in March but dies in November.

1909 The National Association for the Advancement of Colored People, the NAACP, was founded by W. E. B. Du Bois.

1910 Son Elliott is born.

1910 The Roosevelt family moves to Albany, the capital of New York, after Franklin is elected to the state senate.

1912 Woodrow Wilson is elected president.

1913 The Roosevelt family moves to Washington, D.C., after Franklin is appointed assistant secretary of the navy by President Woodrow Wilson.

1914 Son, also named Franklin Jr., is born.

1916 Son John is born.

1916 Jeannette Rankin of Montana becomes the first woman elected to the United States Congress.

1917 On April 6, the United States declares war on Germany, beginning U.S. involvement in World War I.

1918 Eleanor begins work for the American Red Cross.

1918 Eleanor discovers Franklin's affair with Lucy Mercer.

1918 World War I ends on November 11.

1920 Franklin runs as vice president on the Democratic ticket. After he loses, he works as a lawyer in New York.

1920 Women are granted the right to vote upon ratification of the Nineteenth Amendment to the Constitution.

1920 Warren G. Harding is elected president.

1920 Commercial radio begins broadcasting in the United States.

1921 While vacationing at the family's summer home in Canada, Franklin is stricken with polio.

1922 For the next five years, Eleanor is an active participant in progressive organizations such as the Women's Trade Union League, the League of Women Voters, and Women's Division of the New York State Democratic Committee.

1923 Warren G. Harding dies of a heart attack, and Vice President Calvin Coolidge becomes president.

1924 J. Edgar Hoover is appointed to head the FBI.

1926 The radio network NBC begins, followed by CBS the next year.

1927 Eleanor, along with her friend Marion Dickerman, buys the Todhunter School in New York City and begins teaching there.

1927 Charles Lindbergh is the first person to fly nonstop across the Atlantic Ocean.

1927 The first "talking picture," *The Jazz Singer*, is released.

1928 Franklin is elected governor of New York. Eleanor moves to Albany and assists her husband.

1928 Herbert Hoover is elected president.

1929 The stock market crashes, plunging the country into the Great Depression.

1932 Amelia Earhart flies solo across the Atlantic Ocean.

1932 Franklin is elected president of the United States.

1933 Eleanor assumes the role of First Lady. She takes on a number of projects, including advocating for the Arthurdale community, traveling throughout the country to observe the effect and efficiency of New Deal programs, and writing a newspaper column and books.

1933 Adolf Hitler becomes chancellor of Germany.

1934 Eleanor begins advocating for the African American community.

1936 Franklin is elected to his second term as president.

1939 Germany's invasion of Poland starts World War II in Europe.

1939 At the New York World's Fair, Franklin speaks via an invention new to most people, television.

1940 The Germans march through Europe continues.

1940 Franklin wins an unprecedented third term as president.

1941 Japan bombs Pearl Harbor, triggering the U.S. entry into
World War II, fighting against Japan, Germany, and Italy.

1941-1945 World War II rages with battles throughout the world, and
the Holocaust, the systematic murder of Jews and others, moves
into high gear.

1941-1945 Eleanor spends the war years visiting the troops and
promoting the Tuskegee Airmen, an African American unit of
the U.S. Army Air Corps.

1944 Franklin wins a fourth term as president.

1945 Franklin dies in Warm Springs, Georgia, on April 12.

1945 Germany surrenders on May 7, ending the war in Europe.

1945 The United States drops atomic bombs on the Japanese cities
of Hiroshima and Nagasaki. Japan announces its surrender on
August 15, 1945.

1945 President Harry S. Truman appoints Eleanor to the newly
formed United Nations.

1947 Eleanor becomes chair of the Commission on Human Rights
of the United Nations, which issues a Universal Declaration of
Human Rights.

1952 Dwight D. Eisenhower is elected president of the United States.

1952-1957 Eleanor travels the world. Her visits include Israel, India,
Thailand, and the U.S.S.R.

1960 John F. Kennedy is elected president.

1962 Eleanor dies of heart failure after contracting aplastic anemia
and tuberculosis of the bone marrow.

NOTES

PROLOGUE

vi   "even if they had to blow the place up" www.pbs.org/wgbh /americanexperience/features/primary-resources/eleanor-fbi/2/.

vii   Information on the history of the Highlander Folk School can be found at www.tnhistoryforkids.org/history/in-search-of /in-search-of/highlander.2522958.

vii   Information on Eleanor's visit can be found at www.neh.gov /humanities/2000/januaryfebruary/feature/eleanor-roosevelt.

1
Granny

1–2   "My mother was one of the most beautiful . . ." Eleanor Roosevelt, *The Autobiography of Eleanor Roosevelt* (New York: Harper Perennial, reprint edition, 2014) 3.

3   "a miracle from heaven . . ." Joseph P. Lash, *Eleanor and Franklin: The Story of Their Relationship Based on Eleanor Roosevelt's Private Papers.* (New York: W. W. Norton, 1971) 21.

3   "sink through the floor . . ." Roosevelt, *Autobiography,* 9.

3   "ugly" Candace Fleming, *Our Eleanor: A Scrapbook Look at Eleanor Roosevelt's Remarkable Life* (New York: Antheneum Books for Young Readers/Anne Schwartz, 2005).

4   "through the Grand snow-clad forests..." Eric Burns,
     *Someone to Watch Over Me: A Portrait of Eleanor Roosevelt
     and the Tortured Father Who Shaped Her Life* (New York:
     W. W. Norton/Pegasus, 2017) 76 (galley).

4   "With my father..." Roosevelt, *Autobiography*, 5.

6   "a small and ragged urchin" Burns, *Someone*, 12.

8   "somehow it was always..." Roosevelt, *Autobiography*, 9.

9   "I knew in my mind..." Russell Freedman, *Eleanor Roosevelt:
     A Life of Discovery* (New York: Clarion Books, 1993) 15.

10   "We were brought up on the principle..." Roosevelt,
     Autobiography, 6.

10   "Your mother wanted..." Lash, *Eleanor and Franklin*, 73.

11   "Suddenly life..." Roosevelt, *Autobiography*, 20.

11   "Anything I had accomplished..." Lash, *Eleanor and
     Franklin*, 6.

2
Finding Herself

12   "lost and lonely" Roosevelt, *Autobiography*, 20.

12   "eyes looked through you... and she always knew..." Ibid., 22.

14   "courageous judgment..." Lash, *Eleanor and Franklin*, 80.

14   "underdog should..." Ibid., 80.

15–16   "Never again would I be..." Roosevelt, *Autobiography*, 31.

16   "more satisfaction..." Ibid., 29.

18   "Protect yourself..." Blanche Wiesen Cook, *Eleanor Roosevelt:
        Volume 1, The Early Years, 1884–1933* (New York: Penguin,
        1992) 123.

18   "utter agony" Lash, *Eleanor and Franklin*, 93.

19   "She was always..." Cook, *Volume 1*, 128.

22   "misery and exploitation . . ." Lash, *Eleanor and Franklin*, 98.

22   "glow of pride" Freedman, *Eleanor Roosevelt*, 34.

23   "I was appalled . . . I saw little children . . ." Lash, *Eleanor and Franklin*, 100.

3
Losing Herself

25   "Oh! Darling, . . ." Cook, *Volume 1*, 139.

27   "A very good mind" Lash, *Eleanor and Franklin*, 101.

28   "with your help" Ibid., 98.

28   "My God . . ." Ibid., 135.

28–29   "Having been born . . ." Ibid., 119.

29   "good little mother's boy" Ibid., 103.

31   "A few irate guests . . ." Roosevelt, *Autobiography*, 50.

32   "I do not remember . . ." Ibid., 50.

34   "Your mother only bore you . . ." Fleming, *Our Eleanor*, 24.

35   "You were never quite sure . . ." Lash, *Eleanor and Franklin*, 162.

37   "I worried for fear . . ." Roosevelt, *Autobiography*, 63.

38   "Duty was perhaps the motivating force . . ." Ibid., 66.

38   "The first requisite . . ." Cook, *Volume 1*, 191.

38   "She was playing the political game . . ." Lash, *Eleanor and Franklin*, 192.

39   "was not favorably impressed" 67.

40   "felt as if my own son . . ." Cook, *Volume 1*, 197.

41   "May history repeat itself." Ibid., 200.

42   "the men in government . . ." Freedman, *Eleanor Roosevelt: A Life*, 58.

42   "I became a more tolerant person . . ." Roosevelt, *Autobiography*, 93.

4
A Life to Be Lived

48 "Life was meant to be lived" Roosevelt, *Autobiography*, 104.

48–49 "the Southern blood of my ancestors . . ." Cook, *Volume 1*, 251.

49 "The benefits of the war . . ." Ibid., 250.

50 "No words from you . . ." Cook, *Volume 1*, 252.

50 As a young woman . . . One discussion of Eleanor's feelings toward the Jews appears in this book review of *FDR and the Jews* by Richard Breitman and Allan J. Lichtman at jewishstandard.timesofisrael.com/eleanor-roosevelt-and-the -jews but is also mentioned in other sources. Her casual anti-Semitism was a hallmark of America's upper classes and what is remarkable is not her prejudice but her evolution. In *Eleanor Roosevelt: A Life of Discovery*, Russell Freedman comments that Eleanor knew virtually no blacks.

51 "superior creatures" Fleming, *Our Eleanor*, 43.

54 "Have something . . ." Roosevelt, *Autobiography*, 124.

55 "for the intensive education . . ." Roosevelt, *Autobiography*, 113.

56 "You will surely break down . . ." Cook, *Volume 1*, 309.

57 "the intense and devastating influence . . ." Hazel Rowley, *Franklin and Eleanor: An Extraordinary Marriage* (New York: Farrar, Straus and Giroux, 2010) 117.

58 "if he fights . . ." Fleming, *Our Eleanor*, 47.

59 "It began to dawn on me . . ."

61 "And I never forgot . . ." Cook, *Volume 1*, 399.

61 "into an enlivened understanding . . ." Ibid., 405.

61 "I like teaching better . . ." Ibid., 399.

62 "What was the food like . . ." Freedman, *Eleanor Roosevelt: A Life*, 87.

5
Reaching Out

64   "The only thing we have to fear . . ." www.pbs.org/wgbh /americanexperience/features/bonus-video/presidents-enemy-fdr.

69   "Well, all right . . ." Roosevelt, *Autobiography*, 176–177.

70   "Just for one day . . ." Fleming, *Our Eleanor*, 72.

70   "From March 1933 . . . the variety of requests . . ." Roosevelt, *Autobiography*, 171.

71   "a stranded generation" Blanche Wiesen Cook, *Eleanor Roosevelt: Volume 2, The Defining Years, 1933–1938* (New York: Penguin, 1992) 269.

72   "the missus organization" Fleming, *Our Eleanor*, 92.

72   "Out here . . ." Cook, *Volume 2*, 271.

75   "I couldn't believe my eyes . . ." Lash, *Eleanor and Franklin*, 522

76   "*Darky* was used. . ." Ibid., 522.

77   "She was not afraid . . ." jewishstandard.timesofisrael.com /eleanor-roosevelt-and-the-jews.

6
A New Standard for Understanding

80   "thoughtless people . . . just to make . . ." Cook, *Volume 2*, 156.

80–81   "Along the main street . . ." Cook, *Volume 2*, 130.

81–82   "He thinks . . ." Roosevelt, *Autobiography*, 178.

83   "I have always felt . . ." Cook, *Volume 2*, 151

84   "thoroughly opposed . . ." Cook, *Volume 2*, 139.

86   "I can remember . . ." Ibid., 159.

86–87   "Never before . . ." Ibid., 153.

87   "set before all of us . . ." Ibid., 153.

88   "the girl who did not stand up" Patricia Bell-Scott, *The Firebrand and the First Lady: Portrait of a Friendship* (New York: Knopf, 2016) 29.

88   "Twelve millions of your citizens . . ." Ibid., 27.

89   "isn't my problem alone . . ." Ibid., 27.

7
The Spur

91   "carnivals of death" The Editorial Board, "Lynching as Racial Terrorism," *New York Times*, February 11, 2015, www.nytimes.com/2015/02/11/opinion/lynching-as-racial-terrorism.html.

92   "We know that it is murder . . ." Blog of the Franklin D. Roosevelt Presidential Library and Museum; "Eleanor Roosevelt's Battle to End Lynching," blog entry by Paul M. Sparrow, Director, February 12, 2016, fdr.blogs.archives.gov/2016/02/12/eleanor-roosevelts-battle-to-end-lynching/.

93   "The President talked to me . . ." Lash, *Eleanor and Franklin*, 515.

94   Had she coached . . . "Well, at least I know . . ." The incident of the Roosevelt-White meeting is reported in Cook, *Volume 2*, 181.

94   "I did not choose the tools . . ." Ibid., 516.

96   "dynamite" Ibid., 516.

97   "No, certainly not. . . . " Doris Kearns Goodwin, *No Ordinary Time: Franklin and Eleanor Roosevelt—The Home Front in World War II* (New York: Simon & Schuster, 1994) 164.

98   "Of course . . ." Cook, *Volume 2*, 246

98   "in silent rebuke . . ." Blog of the Franklin D. Roosevelt Presidential Library and Museum; "Eleanor Roosevelt's Battle to End Lynching," blog entry by Paul M. Sparrow, Director,

February 12, 2016, fdr.blogs.archives.gov/2016/02/12/eleanor
-roosevelts-battle-to-end-lynching/.

99   "He might have been happier.... Nevertheless..." Roosevelt,
      Autobiography, 279.

8
It Never Hurts to Be Kind

101   Blog of Real-Time News from Birmingham; "The Week in
      Birmingham History: Eleanor Roosevelt Faced Off Against Bull
      Connor." Though reported in a number of books about Eleanor,
      this article gives the fullest account: www.al.com/news
      /birmingham/index.ssf/2014/11/the_week_in_birmingham
      _history_23.html.

102   The insight about Eleanor kissing Mrs. Bethune appears in Lash,
      Eleanor and Franklin, 523, and was reported in an interview he
      conducted with Eleanor's daughter, Anna Roosevelt.

103   "not available to Negro artists." Blanche Wiesen Cook, *Eleanor
      Roosevelt: Volume 3, The War Years and After, 1939–1962*
      (New York: Viking, 2016) 34.

103   "shocked beyond words..." Ibid., 34.

103   "You had the opportunity to lead..." www.pbs.org/wgbh
      /americanexperience/features/biography/eleanor-anderson.

103   "Genius knows no color line" www.youtube.com
      /watch?v=mAONYTMf2pk This clip features highlights
      of the Anderson concert.

105   "a firebrand" Bell-Scott, *The Firebrand*, xviii.

106   "burst into spontaneous laughter" Bell-Scott, *The Firebrand*, 114.

107   "I feel if these girls..." Lois Scharf, *Eleanor Roosevelt: First
      Lady of American Liberalism* (Boston: C.K. Hall, 1987) 107.

107　"Surely you would not . . ." Lash, *Eleanor and Franklin*, 521.

109　"I'm not surprised . . ." Roosevelt, *Autobiography*, 193.

110　"develop skin as tough as a rhinoceros hide" Fleming, *Our Eleanor*, 104.

9
War Clouds

114　Religious and racial prejudice "are a great menace . . ." Cook, *Volume 3*, 248.

115　"Eleanor refused to be insulated . . ." Lash, *Volume 3, 521*.

115　"It seems incredible . . . Cook, *Volume 3*, 34.

117　"Hell, if you said you were colored . . ." Goodwin, *No Ordinary Time*, 166.

117　"Our main reason for writing . . ." Ibid., 167.

118　"You know, better than any other people . . . the road to better understanding . . . faith and cooperation . . ." Cook, *Volume 3*, 357.

118　"This is going to be very bad politically . . ." Lash, *Eleanor and Franklin*, 530.

118　"a commanding figure" Goodwin, *No Ordinary Time*, 161.

119　"emphasized that . . ." Cook, *Volume 3*, 362.

120　"experiments which would . . ." Goodwin, *No Ordinary Time*, 169.

121　"The policy of the War Department . . . This policy . . . to make changes . . ." Cook, *Volume 3*, 363.

122　"vague and general language" Bell-Scott, *The Firebrand*, 100.

122　"imperialism" Ibid., 100.

123–23　"I wonder if it ever occurred to you . . . your letter . . ." Ibid., 101.

123　"desperation and disgust." Ibid., 102.

123　"militant armor . . ." Ibid., 102.

124   "Negroes will be considered only . . ." Goodwin, *No Ordinary Time*, 246.

126   "the first official call . . ." Ibid., 249.

126   "Negroes up to a certain percentage . . ." Ibid., 249.

127   "We want you to issue an executive order . . ." Ibid., 249.

127   "to provide for the full and equitable participation . . ." Ibid., 252.

10
Fighting and Dying

128   "A date which will live in infamy" www.youtube.com /watch?v=W6ScDXwYjWA.

129   "I imagine every mother . . ." Fleming, *Our Eleanor*, 115.

130   "I kept being appalled . . ." Goodwin, *No Ordinary Time*, 274.

130   "My idea of hell . . ." Cook, *Volume 3*, 427.

131–32   "the bitterness . . . objectively . . . for the honor . . ." www.nps .gov/articles/erooseveltinternment.htm.

133   "One of the things . . ." jewishstandard.timesofisrael.com/eleanor -roosevelt-and-the-jews.

136   "We liked this speech . . ." Goodwin, *No Ordinary Time*, 463.

136   "She did more good . . ." Ibid., 465.

136–37   "coddling of Negroes . . . I suppose . . ." Ibid., 446.

137   "sound patronizing" Lash, *Eleanor and Franklin*, 676.

138   "These colored boys . . ." Goodwin, *No Ordinary Time*, 522.

140   "Your letters and gifts . . ." Fleming, *Our Eleanor*, 123.

140   "there's a private down here . . ." docs.fdrlibrary.marist.edu /images/p7742.jpg.

142   "In my heart . . ." Cook, *Volume 3*, 575.

142   "He did his job . . ." www.nytimes.com/learning/general /onthisday/big/0412.html?mcubz=0.

143 "Goin' Home" time.com/photography/life/.

144 "Is there anything . . ." Goodwin, *No Ordinary Time*, 605.

144 "The only limit . . ." Cook, *Volume 3*, 577.

144 "The story is over" Fleming, *Our Eleanor*, 131.

11
Turning the Page

145 "with fear and trembling" Eleanor Roosevelt, *On My Own: The Years Since the White House* (New York: Harper & Brothers, 1958) 299.

146 "that as the only woman . . ." Fleming, *Our Eleanor*, 135.

148 "I want to take back . . ." Joseph P. Lash, *Eleanor: The Years Alone* (New York: W. W. Norton, 1972) 47.

152 "insistence that there be no hatred in this struggle" kingencyclopedia.stanford.edu/encyclopedia/encyclopedia /enc_roosevelt_anna_eleanor_1884_1962.

152 "The impact of her personality . . ." Epitaph for Mrs. FDR. *New York Amsterdam News*, November 24, 1962.

153 "Staying aloof . . ." www.gwu.edu/~erpapers/teachinger/lesson -plans/notes-er-and-civil-rights.cfm.

154 "And here they are . . ." www. neh. gov/humanities/2000 /januaryfebruary/feature/ Eleanor Roosevelt.

155 "The great lesson . . ." Bell-Scott, *The Firebrand*, 352.

155 "You gain strength . . ." Eleanor Roosevelt, *You Learn by Living: Eleven Keys for a More Fulfilling Life* (New York: Harper Perennial, reprint edition, 2016).

BIBLIOGRAPHY

*Denotes books of interest for young people

BOOKS

Bell-Scott, Patricia. *The Firebrand and the First Lady: Portrait of a Friendship*. New York: Knopf, 2016.

Burns, Eric. *Someone to Watch Over Me: A Portrait of Eleanor Roosevelt and the Tortured Father Who Shaped her Life*. New York: W. W. Norton/Pegasus, 2017. (Galley)

Cook, Blanche Wiesen. *Eleanor Roosevelt: Volume 1, The Early Years, 1884–1933*. New York: Penguin, 1992.

———. *Eleanor Roosevelt: Volume 2, The Defining Years, 1933–1938*. New York: Penguin, 1999.

———. *Eleanor Roosevelt: Volume 3, The War Years and After, 1939–1962*. New York: Viking, 2016.

*Fleming, Candace. *Our Eleanor: A Scrapbook Look at Eleanor Roosevelt's Remarkable Life*. New York: Atheneum Books for Young Readers/Anne Schwartz, 2005.

*Freedman, Russell. *Eleanor Roosevelt: A Life of Discovery*. New York: Clarion Books, 1993.

Gerber, Robin. *Leadership the Eleanor Roosevelt Way: Timeless Strategies from the First Lady of Courage*. Portfolio, 2003.

Goodwin, Doris Kearns. *No Ordinary Time: Franklin and Eleanor*

Roosevelt—The Home Front in World War II. New York:
Simon & Schuster, 1994.

Lash, Joseph P. *Eleanor: The Years Alone*. New York: W. W. Norton,
1972.

——. *Eleanor and Franklin: The Story of Their Relationship Based
on Eleanor Roosevelt's Private Papers*. New York: W.W. Norton,
1971.

Roosevelt, Eleanor. *On My Own: The Years Since the White House*.
New York: Harper & Brothers, 1958.

——. Chadakoff, Rochelle, ed. *Eleanor Roosevelt's My Day:
Her Acclaimed Columns 1936–1945*. Seattle: Pharos Books, 1989.

——. *The Autobiography of Eleanor Roosevelt*. New York:
Harper Perennial, reprint edition, 2014.

——. *You Learn by Living: Eleven Keys for a More Fulfilling Life*.
New York: Harper Perennial, reprint edition, 2016.

Rowley, Hazel. *Franklin and Eleanor: An Extraordinary Marriage*.
New York: Farrar, Straus and Giroux, 2010.

Scharf, Lois. *Eleanor Roosevelt: First Lady of American Liberalism*.
Boston: C.K. Hall, 1987.

WEBSITES

Eleanor Roosevelt and the Jews: jewishstandard.timesofisrael.com
/eleanor-roosevelt-and-the-jew

New Deal Network: newdeal.feri.org/index.htm

Week in Birmingham History: www.al.com/news/birmingham/index...
/the_week_in_birmingham_history

National Archives Forward with Roosevelt—the blog of the Franklin
Delano Roosevelt Presidential Library and Museum: fdr.blogs
.archives.gov/2016/02/12/eleanor-roosevelts-battle-to-end-lynching

BIBLIOGRAPHY

Marian Anderson sings at Lincoln Memorial: www.youtube.com
/watch?v=mAONYTMf2pk

The King Center/Eleanor Roosevelt: kingencyclopedia.stanford
.edu/encyclopedia/encyclopedia/enc_roosevelt_anna
_eleanor_1884_1962

Eleanor Roosevelt/Humanities: www.neh.gov/humanities/2000
/januaryfebruary/feature/eleanor-roosevelt

Tennessee History for Kids: www.tnhistoryforkids.org/places
/highlander

Speech to Congress, December 8, 1941: www.youtube.com
/watch?v=W6ScDXwYjWA

Eleanor Roosevelt: Undo the Mistake of Internment: www.nps.gov
/articles/erooseveltinternment.htm

New York Times: www.nytimes.com/learning/general/onthisday
/big/0412.html?mcubz=0

AUTHOR'S NOTE

When I began writing this book, I thought I knew a good deal about Eleanor Roosevelt. Certainly, I was aware of her unhappy childhood, the ways in which her husband's extramarital affair affected her personal relationships, and how her unrelenting work as First Lady had bought her both high praise and intense vilification. I also knew that one of her great interests was in the civil rights movement.

What I didn't know was how late Eleanor came to her involvement in this cause. It was not until 1933, as Franklin Roosevelt began his first term as president during the Depression, that she began to understand the corrosive effects of the United States' subjugation of its black citizens. Eleanor came to see how detrimental this bigotry was to both African Americans and the country as a whole. In the process, she became more aware of her own feelings and prejudices.

This is the story of Eleanor's evolution—how she used her megaphone and access to power to help those already on the front lines of social justice movements further their causes. At various points in her life, Eleanor Roosevelt was broken and had to remake herself. It was this growth that allowed her to evolve and to realize that she shared a common humanity with those determined to secure their inalienable rights. Fighting injustice became her life's work.

Note: I struggled with which names to use for the people in this book. It seemed almost too forward to call Eleanor Roosevelt by her first name, especially later in life. But Eleanor the girl—the one who was orphaned and often fearful but tried hard to do her best—remained an important part of the woman she became, so I primarily use Eleanor throughout. Consequently, for the most part, I also use first names for others.

ACKNOWLEDGMENTS

It is always a pleasure to work with Abrams Books for Young Readers because of the care and diligence the staff put into each book. I'm particularly grateful to my editor, the smart, savvy Howard Reeves, who keeps pushing in the best possible way; and to the awesome Emily Daluga, whose patience is endless and her ability to keep the train on the track is remarkable. Abrams is known for its beautiful book making and here the thanks go to associate art director Pamela Notarantonio and the book's designer Sara Corbett. I would also like to thank the staff at the Franklin D. Roosevelt Presidential and Museum in Hyde Park, New York, especially archivist Patrick Fahy, whose help with locating the book's many photographs was invaluable. A special appreciation to Lila Freeman and Vic Glazer who drove me to Hyde Park—in a blizzard!—and, as always, to my husband, Bill Ott, for his support and the endless cups of tea.

INDEX

Note: Page numbers in *italics* refer to illustrations.